The

Yugoslavi

THE
VISITOR'S GUIDE TO
YUGOSLAVIA:
the ADRIATIC COAST

MPC

HUNTER
PUBLISHING INC

British Library Cataloguing in
Publication Data:
Eisenhardt, Jost
    The visitor's guide to Yugoslavia:
    the Adriatic Coast.— (MPC
    visitor's guides).
    1. Yugoslavia— Description and
    travel — 1971-
    I. Title
    914.97'0423   DR1224

Author: Jost Eisenhardt
Translator: Andrew Shackleton

© Goldstadtverlag Karl A. Schäfer,
    Pforzheim
© Moorland Publishing Co Ltd
    1987 (English edition)

Published by:
Moorland Publishing Co Ltd,
Moor Farm Road,
Airfield Estate,
Ashbourne,
Derbyshire DE6 1HD
England

ISBN 0 86190 186 X (paperback)
ISBN 0 86190 187 8 (hardback)

Published in the USA by:
Hunter Publishing Inc.,
300 Raritan Centre Parkway,
CN94, Edison, NJ 08818

ISBN 1 55650 008 4

Printed in the UK by Buxton Press
Ltd, Buxton, Derbyshire

Cover photograph:The Island of
Korcula (Peter Baker, International
Photobank).

Photographs of the Velebit range;
church spire, narrow streets and
fortress at Dubrovnik; Krk viewed
from Cres; Kotor; Krk town; Baska;
Vrbnik and Plitvice National Park
were kindly supplied by R. Scholes.
The remaining photographs were
supplied by the Yugoslav National
Tourist Office.

CONTENTS

FOREWORD

The Adriatic Coast has always been a holiday area, as is shown by the many older villas and hotels that are to be found there. But it was originally a place for the solitary traveller or the privileged few, and few of the towns along the coast were well known, except perhaps Opatija, Crikvenica, Hvar or Dubrovnik.

The situation has changed enormously since then, with the building of new roads, new hotels and new holiday villas. The prices are fairly low, making it a popular holiday destination for people of all nationalities and classes.

In spite of the advances of recent decades, it is not always plain sailing for visitors. Things are done differently from other countries, while even the most recently built roads often have a surprising number of potholes. And some of the many hotels that have sprung up are no longer in perfect condition.

However, this is amply compensated by the beauty of the scenery and the friendliness and colourfulness of the people. An Adriatic holiday can indeed be a truly unforgettable experience.

Tours, Towns and Cities

The touring section (Chapters 1–4) describes the journey down the coast that a motorist might take, beginning in the north and gradually working his way southwards. Chapter 5 gives a more detailed account of the main towns, islands and other attractions along the way. They are given in alphabetical order for the sake of simplicity, and are indicated elsewhere in the text by means of an asterisk (*).

Place Names

The place names used in this guide are the Serbo-Croat or Slovene names that are current in modern Yugoslavia. However, many places are still occasionally known by the old names that they were given by their former rulers, whether Austrian or Venetian. Thus many of the towns along the coast have old Italian names (such as Fiume for Rijeka), while some of those inland have old German names (such as Adelsberg for Postojna). Where appropriate the old names are given in brackets after the modern ones, and sometimes in Chapter 5 a cross-reference has been given.

Key to Symbols Used in Margin

 Museum/Art Gallery

 Archaeological Site

 Building of Interest

Castle/Fortification

Church/Ecclesiastical Site

 Gardens

 View/Natural Phenomenon

Nature Reserve/Zoo

Parkland

Other Places of Interest

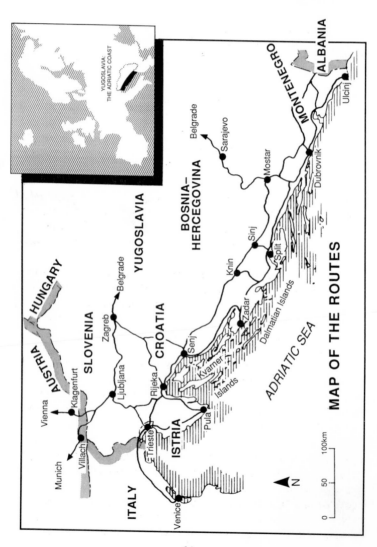

MAP OF THE ROUTES

YUGOSLAVIA:
THE ADRIATIC COAST

INTRODUCTION

The Country of Yugoslavia

Geography

Yugoslavia has an area of 256,000sq km, making it somewhat larger than Britain and slightly larger than the American state of Oregon. But its population of 23 million is less than half that of the United Kingdom. The country is bounded by Austria and Hungary to the north, Rumania and Bulgaria to the east, and Greece and Albania to the south. The short border with Italy runs through the Julian Alps to the north-west, while the west side of the country is mostly bounded by the Adriatic.

Yugoslavia is primarily a country of mountains, which cover about three-quarters of the total land surface. The largest range is the Dinaric Alps that border the Adriatic Coast. They form a single chain in the north-west around Trieste, but further south they broaden out into a complex system of mountain chains, which in Serbia are about 250km wide.

The northern border runs through several ranges that form part of the Alps proper, including the Karawanken and the Julian Alps. The Julian Alps run south towards the Adriatic, forming a link with the Dinaric Alps; among them is the Triglav, which with a height of 2,863m (9,390ft) is the highest peak in Yugoslavia.

One special feature of the Yugoslavian mountains is a type of scenery known as *karst*. The original Karst (Krst) is a region of barren plateaux overlooking Trieste in north-western Yugoslavia. It is full of strange limestone formations that are also to be found in other parts of the Dinaric Alps. The word karst has thus become a geographical term referring to all instances of this type of scenery.

Karst scenery results from the erosion of a particular kind of

11

The Julian Alps run south towards the Adriatic

limestone that is full of joints and fissures. Rainwater drains away through these fissures, and gradually dissolves the limestone away. The result is a complex system of rills, sinkholes, basins and caves. Some of the associated phenomena have strange technical names such as karren, dolines and poljes. The most famous of the caves are those at Postojna in the Karst region itself.

Apart from these areas of barren karst, the mountains are mostly covered with forests. Yugoslavia has a higher proportion of forest than any other Mediterranean country.

The Velebit range, Dinaric Alps

At the northern end of the Adriatic Coast is the peninsula of Istria. Its highest point is the Ucka (1,396m (4,579ft)); this long mountain barrier overlooks the Kvarner Riviera on the east side of the peninsula, protecting the coastline from cold northerly winds. The west side is rather gentler and covered with forest, and there are numerous small islands off the coast.

The Dinaric Alps are made up of numerous constituent ranges. Those along the coast include the Velebit, the Dinara, the Kozjak, the Mosor and the Biokovo. They form a barrier along the coastline, protecting it from the cold winds of the interior. They are often barren, with large areas of karst forming an impressive contrast to the blue of the sea and the green of the fertile coastal strip. The sea often forms inlets that run a long way inland. The coastal plain is very narrow, with only a few breaches in the mountains leading to the inland regions of Bosnia and Hercegovina.

The Dalmatian Coast is particularly irregular; it extends from Karlobag in the north to the Gulf of Kotor in the south, and its total length is three times the equivalent distance as the crow flies. There are a few broad, sandy beaches on the Croatian Coast further north (such as Crikvenica). The innumerable beaches of Dalmatia are

The Island of Krk, viewed from Cres

mostly in small bays and coves, and covered with stones and shingle. There are more than 400 small harbours dotted along the coast.

The numerous offshore islands are geographically very interesting. They are formed into long chains and have steep coastlines, showing that they are structurally part of the Dinaric mountain range. The sea level has risen, turning the valleys into channels and the mountains into islands. There are more than 1000 islands if one includes every islet and rock. But only about seventy of the larger islands are actually inhabited. The largest is Krk, with an area of 409sq km. Many of the best seaside resorts are to be found on the larger islands, while some of the small ones make fascinating places to visit.

The only lowland region of Yugoslavia is in the north-east bordering on Hungary and Rumania. This fertile basin is drained by the Danube (Dunav) and its tributaries, the Drava, the Sava, the Tisa and the Morava. It is liable to dangerous flooding, especially from the fast-flowing Drava and Sava.

Geographically speaking then, Yugoslavia is a land of great variety, with high mountains and bare limestone karst, broad forests and narrow coastal plains, lush valleys and broad grasslands.

The Moraca Valley, Montenegro

The Political Divisions

The geographical variety is also reflected in the political make-up of the country. For the Socialist Federal Republic of Yugoslavia is made up of no less than six constituent republics.

The most northerly of these is Slovenia (Slovenija), with an area of 20,250sq km and a population of 1.9 million. The capital, Ljubljana, has a population of some 305,000. The scenery is varied, with the mighty Julian Alps in the west (Triglav; 2,863m (9,390ft)) and gentle hill country to the east. Slovenia is an important wine-growing region. The two main tourist centres are the mountain resort of Bled and Postojna, famous for its caves. There are several seaside resorts along the tiny coastal strip running from Portoroz to the Italian border.

The constituent republic of Croatia (Hrvatska) has an area of 56,500sq km and a population of 4.6 million. Its capital is Zagreb, with a population of 1,174,500. Apart from Croatia proper, it includes most of the peninsula of Istria and the whole of the coastal province of Dalmatia extending as far south as the Gulf of Kotor. The Dalmatian Coast is one of the most interesting regions of Yugoslavia from the tourist's point of view.

The southern part of the coast belongs to Montenegro (Crna

Mountainous scenery of western Slovenia

Gora), which with an area of only 14,000sq km is the smallest of the constituent republics. The capital Titograd has a population of only 132,000. The Montenegrins are a proud mountain race with a long history. The name of their country means 'black mountain', and the highest peak is the Durmitor (2,522m (8,272ft)).

The constituent republic of Bosnia–Hercegovina (Bosna i Hercegovina) has an area of 51,150sq km and a population of just 4.1 million. The capital Sarajevo has about 500,000 inhabitants.

Bosnia–Hercegovina is bounded by Montenegro to the south and by the narrow coastal strip of Dalmatia to the west. The west of the region consists mostly of barren karst, while to the east it becomes increasingly wooded, with a thriving forestry industry. The gentle hill country to the north is a major plum growing area.

Visitors to the coast are strongly recommended to make an excursion into this fascinating region, where a large part of the population is Moslem. The mosques with their minarets and the Turkish-style buildings give the towns and villages an oriental atmosphere.

The most southerly of the constituent republics is Macedonia (Makedonija). It has an area of 25,700sq km and a population of 1.9 million. In the past Macedonia has been a somewhat disputed region,

The Dalmatian Coast

having no natural boundaries, either with Bulgaria in the east or Albania in the west. Being isolated and mountainous, it has tended to remain underdeveloped; but strenuous efforts are now being made to bring it into line with the other regions. The capital, Skopje, is growing fast, and with a population of 506,000 is now larger than Sarajevo.

Macedonia is well known for the wonderful architecture of its monasteries. Lake Ohrid in the south is one of the most beautiful lakes in the whole of Europe. It straddles the Albanian border, and its unspoiled shores are a bather's paradise. Also on the Albanian border is Yugoslavia's second-highest peak, the Korab (2,764m (9,065ft)).

Serbia (Srbija) is by far the largest of the constituent republics, with an area of 88,350sq km and a population of 9.3 million including its two provinces (see below). The capital, Belgrade (Beograd), is also the capital of Yugoslavia, and has a population of 1.5 million. Serbia also includes two socialist autonomous provinces: Vojvodina (Novi Sad) in the north adjoining Hungary and Romania, and Kosovo (Pristina) in the south adjoining Albania.

Much of Serbia is mountainous, and the Morava is the main river running through it. The south is a region of alternating mountains and river basins. There is a large group of monasteries in the central area between Kragujevac and Nis. The northern region of Vojvodina consists of a fertile lowland plain. The main agricultural products are fruit, wine and wheat.

This summary of the different regions shows the enormous variety of scenery to be found in Yugoslavia. But the most beautiful parts of the country are undoubtedly the areas along the coast.

Fauna and Flora

The most interesting feature of the coastal vegetation is the strong contrast between barren karst and lush forests. The peninsula of Istria is covered with rich vegetation; the same is also true of the Vinodol region around Novi, the Kastelanski Riviera near Split, the coast between Brela and Makarska, the lower valley of the Neretva near Metkovic, the area around Dubrovnik, and finally some of the islands.

The vegetation in the north is similar to that of Central Europe, but it becomes gradually more exotic as one travels down the coast. There are palms, cypresses, agaves, oleanders and opuntias. Typical fruit trees include the olive, the fig, the laurel, the mulberry, the pomegranate, the carob and the strawberry-tree. There are sweet chestnuts, cedars, maritime pines, and even oranges and lemons, while vines seem to flourish all over the place.

The countryfolk make great efforts at cultivation, even in the karst regions, where the mountain slopes are often covered with a dense layer of undergrowth. Common plants in these areas include myrtle, rosemary, pistachio and juniper, and one can sometimes find whole fields full of lavender.

The fauna is most interesting in the mountain fastnesses of the interior, where bears and wolves are still to be found. Local farmers claim that in cold winters these animals sometimes come right down to the coast. Roe deer, hares and wild boars are to be found

Lush forests at Brela, typical of coastal vegetation

everywhere. The chamois lives in the mountains of Velebit, the jackal on Korcula and Peljesac and in the area around Bar.

One especially interesting animal is the mongoose, which was introduced by sailors to the island of Mljet to keep down the snake population. Snakes are common in the south, and tortoises are equally abundant. The karst caves contain yet another special animal called an olm — a whitish or reddish salamander that can grow up to 30cm (12in) long.

The birdlife of Yugoslavia is both interesting and varied. The lakes and marshes in areas such as the mouth of the Neretva are the habitat for a large number of water birds, including swans, pelicans, herons and rails.

The Yugoslavian coast is a marvellous place for fish. Many of the local sea fish are on display in the fish markets or available in local restaurants. There are sea perch, turbot, sole, mackerel, tunny, eel, anchovy, cuttlefish, lobster and oysters, just to name but a few.

Shore fishing is still practised near Sibenik, while the waters around the Kornat Islands are a paradise for underwater fishing.

Dolphins can often be seen from boats. One less pleasant form of sea life is a dangerous (to man) species of shark. Coasts and beaches normally have a system for warning bathers of approaching sharks, but it is nevertheless advisable not to swim too far out to sea.

The People of Yugoslavia

Yugoslavia is a country of many different races, of which the great majority are of Slavic origin. The largest group are the Serbs, of whom there are about 9 million; they live mostly in Serbia, but also form the majority in Bosnia–Hercegovina. The Croats number about 5 million; they live primarily in Croatia, but some also live in Bosnia–Hercegovina. There are some 2 million Slovenes in Slovenia, while $1^{1}/_{2}$ million Macedonians and 500,000 Montenegrins each form the majority in their respective constituent republics. The Macedonians and Slovenes each have their own language, while the other three races speak Serbo-Croat.

The largest of the non-Slavic groups consists of some 2 million Albanians; they are mostly concentrated in the autonomous province of Kosovo, but also live in Montenegro and Macedonia. Hungarians form a significant group (400,000) in the autonomous province of Vojvodina. Other smaller minorities include Turks, Bulgarians and Slovaks (two more Slavic peoples), Italians, Rumanians and Germans, not forgetting the many gypsies that live in the south

As far as the coastal regions are concerned, there are Slovenes along the short length of coast north of Savudrija, while the tiny Italian minority live mostly in towns on the west side of Istria. The rest of Istria, Croatia and Dalmatia belong mostly to the Croats, though some Serbs are to be found in Dalmatia. The southern part of the coast is inhabited mainly by Montenegrins, though there are Albanians living in the area around Ulcinj, and even a small Yugoslavian black minority (descendants of slaves).

The ethnic variety is reflected in the religious practices of Yugoslavia. About a third of the population are Roman Catholic, these being for the most part Slovenes and Croats. About half the population are Eastern Orthodox; these consist mostly of Serbs, Montenegrins and Macedonians, and belong to the Serbian and Macedonian

Orthodox churches. Then there is a significant Moslem minority (2 million), most of them Albanians and Turks living in Macedonia and especially in Kosovo. Under Turkish rule Islam spread north through Montenegro, and across the whole of Bosnia–Hercegovina, where the Moslems form a large minority to this day. Finally, Protestants and Jews form two further small minorities.

Traditional Costume and Folklore

The variation in traditional costumes again reflects the many different cultural influences of the past. The costume in Slovenia has an Alpine feel to it, with leather shorts and dirndl dresses. The Venetian influence is very obvious in the northern coastal areas, especially along the west coast of Istria. The costumes are simpler and more modest along the Croatian coast, but gradually become more colourful and elaborate as one travels down the coast. The finest costumes

Folk-dancing in traditional costume

Colourful national costume, near Dubrovnik

are those to be found in the Konavlije Valley, just south of Dubrovnik.

The women wear white dresses, embroidered blouses, short waistcoats and small red caps. Sometimes one can detect a Turkish influence, especially in Bosnia–Hercegovina. The style is generally more oriental as one travels down the coast. Traditional Balkan footwear is similarly oriental in flavour — flat, sandal-like shoes, turned up and pointed at the toes, and often with decorative straps.

Evenings of traditional dancing and folklore are staged for tourists throughout the high season. Most of them are organised by state dance troops at the chief holiday centres. Traditional costumes can also be seen at the many folk-dance events that are held throughout the summer in towns and villages all along the coast. They are normally associated with market days or religious festivals. The most popular dance is the *kolo*, which is Yugoslavia's national dance.

The following places are particularly famous for their costume dancing: Obrovac (about 30km from Starigrad-Paklenica and 51km from Zadar), Trebinje, Kotor, Bar, Stari Bar and Ulcinj. In these places dances are normally held in association with Thursday markets. Sinj and Vrlika (near Split) have dances on Sundays and religious festivals. The beautiful costumes of the Konavlije Valley (near Cavtat) are displayed on market days at Dubrovnik. On the island of Susak next to Losinj, the women still wear their traditional costume at all religious festivals.

During July and August there are music festivals at Split and Dubrovnik. These include performances of music, ballet and drama, plus a variety of folk-music and dancing events. Other interesting folk celebrations include...

in April: the *Kumpanija* at Blato on the island of Korcula;
in July: the Moreska at Korcula on the same island;
in July and August: a festival on the island of Gospa od skrpjela in the Gulf of Kotor;
August: a festival on the island of Krk; August: the Alka Festival at Sinj.

Folk culture, alas, is becoming increasingly confined to museums, but folk crafts are still encouraged in the more traditional country regions. The products make ideal souvenirs, and include lacework, embroidery, tapestry work, wood carvings, shoes, drinking bottles and beakers.

A Short History

The Yugoslavian coast is known to have been settled in prehistoric times. This is proved by discoveries that have been made both on the mainland and on some of the islands. The earliest recorded settlers were the Illyrians, whose territory once stretched from Vienna in the north to Greece in the south, and from the Po in the west to the Morava in the east. One tribe of the Illyrians, the Dalmatians, gave their name to a large portion of the coastline. They were a race of farmers and sailors, and sometimes of pirates as well.

During the period between the seventh and fourth centuries BC, the Greeks founded several small colonies along the Dalmatian coast. These included settlements on islands which they called Pharos (Hvar), Corcyra (Korcula) and Issa (Vis), and the mainland colony of Tragurion (Trogir).

The Romans were the next people to arrive in Illyria. Provoked by repeated attacks from Illyrian pirates, they needed little persuasion to initiate a campaign of conquest. But though they began this in 229 BC, it was nearly 200 years before the process was complete. The Illyrians' fortunes varied, but the Romans gradually gained the upper hand as one tribe after another fell to them. Starting at the coast, they gradually advanced inland, until under Emperor Augustus the whole of Illyria became subject to Rome. The latifundia system was introduced, and urban centres began to appear; in other words, the whole country became Romanised.

'Illyricum' remained a Roman colony for several centuries. The two best-preserved sites from this period are the Roman town of Pola (now called Pula) and the colonial capital of Salona (now Solin near Split). The Emperor Diocletian (AD 284–305), who was born in Dalmatia, took a special interest in the colony. He divided off the south-eastern portion, making it part of a new prefecture, while Istria

Roman temple at Pula

Roman amphitheatre at Pula

and Dalmatia became part of the Italian prefecture. In AD 300 he built his famous palace at Spalato (now called Split).

When the Roman Empire was divided in AD 395, the coastal regions became part of the Western Empire, while the Eastern Empire encompassed areas to the east of a line from Belgrade to Skutari (now Shkodër in Albania). Following the fall of the Western Roman Empire, coastal Dalmatia became part of the Ostrogothic Kingdom under Theodoric. But after his death in 526, it was eventually annexed by the Byzantine Empire.

The Slavs had already arrived in the region from across the Carpathians at the beginning of the fifth century AD. Together with the Avars they made repeated raids on the coast, and the coastal inhabitants retreated into their mountain strongholds. But it was not until the reign of Emperor Heraclius (610–41) that the Slavs took full control of the region, apart from the offshore islands and a few towns along the coast.

The Slovenes moved up into the Alps, and in 788 they transferred their allegiance to the Frankish Kingdom. Their dukes were later replaced by German counts. In the meantime Istria and Dalmatia at first remained under Byzantine rule. But after Charlemagne had conquered the Avars in 800, the Croats also came under Frankish rule.

More than a century later Prince Tomislav succeeded in founding a Croatian Kingdom. However, both he and his successors had problems overcoming the tensions that existed between rival factions in the kingdom, whether among the nobility, between the churches, or between the two main racial groups, the Slavs and the original Roman inhabitants. The power of Croatia increased when the Byzantines gave up their remaining coastal strongholds, but from about AD 1000 these same towns and islands gradually came under the control of Venice.

Meanwhile the Macedonians had formed their own independent state under Tsar Samuel, but after a bitter struggle this was reabsorbed into the Byzantine Empire in 1018. The kings of Croatia died without issue, and their kingdom was subject to further internal strife. In 1102 Croatia was taken over by King Koloman of Hungary.

The Serbs had by now begun a campaign to free themselves from Byzantine rule. In 1217 Stephan, son of the great Serbian conqueror Nemanjas, was crowned king of Serbia. Under his successors Serbia became the leading power in the Balkans. In 1330 the Serbs defeated the Bulgarians in a battle near Velbuzd. King Dusan went on to conquer large areas of Greece, and in 1346 in Skopje he declared himself emperor of Serbia and Greece.

After Dusan's death the Serbian Empire became fragmented into several small principalities, which were no longer able to resist the repeated attacks of the Ottoman Turks. The decisive battle took place in 1389 near Pristina in the Kosovo region, where Prince Lazar of Serbia fell to Murad I, the Turkish sultan. (Pristina remained a Turkish city until 1912.) The Serbs retained some degree of independence by means of clever negotiations, but they could no longer prevent the Turkish advance into Europe. The Turks ruled the inland regions for the next two centuries, and made repeated attempts to wrest the coastal territories from Venice.

At the beginning of the fifteenth century, the Venetians at last managed to gain power over most of the Dalmatian Coast, the one exception being their great rival Ragusa (later Dubrovnik). All the trading and seafaring ports along the coast had been able to profit from the wars between Hungary and Venice. But none more so than Dubrovnik, which remained an independent republic until 1808. Despite all their efforts, the Turks never succeeded in taking the coast. The hinterland changed hands frequently, but most of the coast remained under Venetian control. The Italian influence is visible to this day in towns all along the coast.

In 1697 Prince Eugen beat the Turks in a decisive battle near Zenta, and at the Treaty of Karlowitz in 1699 the Turks were forced to give up part of Croatia and northern Serbia to the Hapsburgs. Thus the Austro-Hungarian Empire became a major power in Europe. As the Turkish power gradually dwindled, the Venetians also pushed their sphere of influence further inland.

Following the fall of Venice, the Treaty of Campo-Formio brought Istria, Slovenia, Dalmatia and Venice itself under Austrian rule. In 1805 these areas were taken over by Napoléon, who brought Istria, Slovenia and Dalmatia together as the Illyrian Provinces. Meanwhile the Russians took over the Gulf of Kotor together with the neighbouring region of Montenegro. This period marked the end of the republic of Dubrovnik, which was taken over by France in 1808.

In 1814, following the fall of Napoléon, the Illyrian Provinces were returned to the Austro-Hungarian Empire, and remained thus for more than a century until the end of World War I. Montenegro became an autonomous principality, while Serbia and Bosnia–Hercegovina remained firmly under Ottoman rule.

The nineteenth century was a period of frequent uprisings against foreign domination. In 1815 there was a Serb rebellion led by Milos Obrenovic; in 1830 he became the leader of an autonomous principality within the Ottoman Empire. In 1836 Serbo-Croat became officially recognised as a written language.

1848 saw the beginning of a nationalist movement further west to create an independent kingdom incorporating Dalmatia, Croatia and Slovenia. In 1869, military recruitments in the Gulf of Kotor provoked another open rebellion. At the Berlin Congress of 1878, the Great Powers recognised Serbia and Montenegro as independent states. In the same year Austria–Hungary occupied the Ottoman territories of Bosnia and Hercegovina. In 1882 Serbia became a kingdom.

Now that Serbia was independent, the Serbian nationalists became all the more determined to liberate those areas still under foreign domination. King Alexander Obrenovic was murdered in 1903, but his successor Peter I (1903–21) continued the struggle. In 1908 Austria–Hungary annexed the occupied territories of Bosnia and Hercegovina, further fuelling the nationalist cause.

Rivalries over territory between the independent Balkan states led to the Second Balkan War. This was resolved in the Treaty of Bucharest in 1913, in which Macedonia was divided between Greece and Serbia. Then in 1914 Archduke Franz Ferdinand of Austria was assassinated in Sarajevo; the event that sparked off World War I.

The end of World War I saw the creation of an independent Yugoslavian (ie South Slav) state uniting the Serbs, the Croats and the Slovenes. They were, however, forced to give up Istria to Italy, together with the islands of Cres, Losinj and Lastovo, and the city of Zadar. This and other tensions led eventually to the assassination of the Croat leader Radic in 1928. The parliament became impotent, and was dissolved by King Alexander, who in 1929 declared Yugoslavia a military dictatorship. In 1934 King Alexander was assassinated in Marseille. A constitutional government was elected, but it was unable to resolve the many political problems that threatened the stability of the country.

*Impressive architectural
legacies of the past*

In 1941, following the outbreak of World War II, Yugoslavia was invaded by the Germans and Italians. They declared Croatia 'independent', and occupied the rest of the country. A Yugoslavian government in exile was established in London, while the occupying forces set up a puppet regime in Belgrade under General Nedic.

In May 1941 a resistance movement was formed under the leadership of a royalist called Draza Mihailovic. The following July saw the formation of another armed resistance movement by the central committee of the Yugoslavian Communist Party. They were called the Partisans, and in 1942 Marshal Josip Broz Tito became their leader. In 1943 the AVNOJ (Anti-Fascist Council for the National Liberation of Yugoslavia) met at Jajce and laid down the constitutional basis for the modern Yugoslav state. In 1944 the capital Belgrade was captured by Soviet and Partisan troops.

An election on 11 November 1945 was followed on 29 November by the proclamation of the Federal People's Republic of Yugoslavia (*Federativna Narodna Republika Jugoslavija* or FNRJ), with Tito as head of government. In 1947 Yugoslavia signed a treaty with Italy in which they regained Zadar and the Slavic portions of Istria. However, the area around Trieste remained disputed territory.

Though communist, Yugoslavia soon came into conflict with the Soviet Union, and in 1949 broke off relations with the Eastern Bloc. Relations were resumed in 1955, but in the meantime further constitutional reforms were introduced in 1952 and 1953. In 1953 Yugoslavia signed the so-called Balkan Pact with Greece and Turkey. In 1954 the Free Territory of Trieste was divided between Italy and Yugoslavia, and Trieste itself went to Italy.

The 1960s was a decade of reform and 1963 saw the introduction of a new constitution, in which the country's name was changed to the Socialist Federal Republic of Yugoslavia (*Socialiticka Federativna Republika Jugoslavija* or SFRJ). The title of President of the Republic was conferred on Tito for life.

A decision to establish a collective presidency in 1971 was prompted by Tito himself who probably realised that his era was entering its final stages — Yugoslavia's public image had been dominated for 25 years or so by Tito's personality and no one person stood out as his successor.

In 1974 a new constitution was introduced which is still in force. It provided for a system of election based on delegations drawn from occupational groups — workers in the social sector; peasants and farm workers; liberal professions (doctors, etc); state officials and soldiers — and territorial constituencies and socio-political groups.

The Federal Assembly consists of two chambers — a Federal Chamber of 220 delegates elected by the Assemblies of the territorial communes and a chamber of Republics and Provinces (eighty-eight delegates) elected by the delegates from the occupational groups. One member from each province or republic is elected for 5 years to the Federal presidency. This collective presidency elects a president and vice-president every year.

The office of President of the Republic was abolished after Tito's death on 4 May 1980.

The immense gathering of world leaders who attended Tito's funeral could be seen as a tribute to both his status as a man and statesman and acknowledgement of Yugoslavia's prominent place in the international community.

Art and Culture

Visitors to the Adriatic Coast of Yugoslavia will not find very much that could be described as art in the modern sense. On the other hand, there is a vast amount of material of cultural and historical interest, especially in Dalmatia.

Little is left from the prehistoric period, though a few ancient items of weaponry, idols and jars have been lovingly preserved in many of the local museums. There are some marvellous examples from the New Stone Age in the Provincial Museum at Sarajevo, the National Museum in Belgrade and the Pristina Museum; while the Ljubljana Museum contains some fascinating Iron Age urns.

Little is left either from the early Greek settlements on the coast and on a few of the islands. The museum at Trogir contains a few tombstones and inscriptions, and a well preserved relief showing Kairos, the Greek god of the opportune moment. The best-known Greek site is on the island of Vis, known to the Greeks and Romans as Issa. But the finest remains were found at Budva on the coast of Montenegro and in Macedonia; these are on view at the National Museum in Belgrade and at the Skopje Museum.

Much remains of the massive structures built during the Roman period. Probably the best example is the ancient Roman city of Pola (now Pula). The amphitheatre is still used for dramatic performances today. Apart from that, there are two triumphal arches, the Porta Aurea and the Porta Gemina, and finally a temple.

Then there is the famous temple of the Emperor Diocletian at Split (formerly Spalato). This massive structure was built for him in about AD 300. It is so enormous that 3,000 people live within its walls today. The ancient palace cellars were discovered only a few years ago. Now that they have been cleaned out, they give a marvellous impression of what the building must have been like originally.

Equally impressive is the nearby site of the ancient colonial capital of Salona (now Solin). Excavations have revealed the foundations of the city walls, the baths, an amphitheatre and a temple.

A mosaic from a Roman villa was discovered at Risan, and a Roman theatre has been preserved at Stobi in Macedonia. Many local museums contain further examples of Roman sculptures and sarcophagi, and of jewellery and other items found in Roman tombs. Tthe best collections are at Pula, Zadar, Split, Zagreb and Belgrade.

Salona also provides some of the richest examples of early Christian culture. Apart from the foundations of several churches and the sarcophagi of Christian martyrs (mostly opened), there is a well preserved fifth-century basilica. The most impressive building from this period is the sixth-century Euphrasius Basilica at Porec. Its valuable mosaics are surpassed only by those at Ravenna — although unlike the Ravenna mosaics they are allowed to be photographed.

The earliest examples of Slavic architecture on the coast are from the ninth century AD. They include the small church of Sveta Barbara at Trogir, and the magnificent church of Sveti Donat at Zadar. Later examples are the churches of Sveti Mihajlo (St Michael) at Ston (near Dubrovnik) and of Sveti Kriz (St Cross) at Nin. These buildings contain stone friezes, often decorated with a variety of wickerwork designs. The museums mentioned above also contain a variety of statues and jewellery from this period.

Sveti Mihajlo at Ston contains the earliest example of a fresco. Most frescos date from the tenth and eleventh centuries. The finest frescos in Yugoslavia are in the church of Sveta Sofija at Ohrid in Macedonia. This church is one of best examples of the Byzantine architecture which flourished in the tenth century, especially in Macedonia. In the rest of Yugoslavia the Byzantine style is mixed with

Sveta Marije, Zadar

the later Romanesque style of architecture. Two examples of this are St George's church near Novi Pazar and the abbey church at Studenica in Serbia.

From the twelfth century onwards, the Romanesque style began to dominate, a good example being the church of Sveti Krsevan at Zadar. Later examples of thirteenth-century Romanesque architecture are Zadar Cathedral and the west portal of Trogir Cathedral. The

Religious painting flourished, especially in Serbia and Macedonia

latter was sculpted by Radovan, and is considered the most beautiful of its kind in the whole of Yugoslavia. What Radovan achieved in stone, Buvina was able to match as a sculptor in wood; his greatest masterpiece is the wooden entrance door of Split Cathedral, which is decorated with twenty-eight reliefs.

Some of the coastal villages possess secular statues from the same period. The thirteenth century was not only a time of cathedral building, but also saw the first examples of a new kind of free-standing bell tower or campanile. The finest such towers in Dalmatia are to be found in the town of Rab and at Split. The bell tower at Split took around 400 years to reach its present form.

The Gothic style of architecture arrived on the Dalmatian Coast at the beginning of the fourteenth century. The most impressive example is the Franciscan monastery at Dubrovnik, with its beautiful cloister created by Miho of Bar. Many of the statues attached to old village houses date back to the same period. Gothic sculpture is also found in the cathedrals at Zadar, Trogir and Kotor, and on the pulpit in Split Cathedral.

The painting of icons also flourished during this period, especially

Franciscan monastery, Dubrovnik

in Serbia and Macedonia. Some of the best examples are in St Clement's Church at Ohrid and in the National Museum at Skopje. In the coastal regions much gold and silverwork was produced for the treasuries of monasteries and churches; two of the best collections of these are at Zadar and Dubrovnik. In the meantime the Bogomil sect of Bosnia–Hercegovina produced large tombstones with strange primitive designs called *stecci* that can still be seen in cemeteries today. Some of the finest examples are outside the Provincial Museum in Sarajevo.

Venetian architecture gradually spread down the coast, one of the best examples being the town hall at Koper (Capodistria). The town of Dubrovnik has an especially rich heritage, with its fortifications, palaces and churches. Apart from its Gothic structures, there are plentiful examples of Renaissance architecture: the Governor's Palace, built in the mid-fifteenth century, the cloister of the Dominican monastery, the west door of the Franciscan monastery and the early sixteenth-century church of Sveti Spas (St Saviour).

Sibenik Cathedral is a particularly impressive example of fifteenth-century Renaissance architecture. Some of Dalmatia's greatest masters took part in its construction, including Juraj Dalmatinac, Andrija Alesi and Nikola Firentinac (ie from Florence). Another pearl of the Renaissance is the chapel of Sveti Ivan (St John) in Trogir Cathedral. The nearby Cipiko Palace is a secular example of Venetian Gothic architecture.

Painting flourished in Dalmatia in the fifteenth century, and schools of art developed in major towns such as Dubrovnik. The best-known masters were Nikola Bozidarovic and Mihajlo Hamzic, both of whose works are on display in Dubrovnik.

The later Turkish advances had a dampening effect on artistic creativity. The Turks built very little on the coast, because they never gained a firm foothold there. However, a mosque remains at Klis, just inland from Split. Other buildings and paintings from the sixteenth and seventeenth centuries are the work of Venetians. They include numerous paintings by Titian and the loggias at Hvar and Zadar, both of which were built by Sanmicheli.

Local art and architecture flourished again at the end of the seventeenth century, when the Baroque style was at its height. At Dubrovnik, which had been destroyed by an earthquake in 1667, a new

Ancient architecture, Omis

cathedral and a Jesuit church were built. But the best example from this period is the tiny town of Perast on the Gulf of Kotor.

Native artists flourished during the centuries which followed, but nothing of great worth was produced. Most artists simply followed the style of their Austrian capital Vienna, though other European styles are also to be found. It was not until the present century that a true

Coastal Yugoslavia enjoys a 'Mediterranean' climate

native style developed. Probably the most important modern Yugoslavian artist is the painter and sculptor Ivan Mestrovic (1883–1962), whose works are on display in the Mestrovic Museum at Split.

Climate and Travel

The coast of Yugoslavia and the islands along it can be visited at any time of year. But while coastal Yugoslavia enjoys a typically Mediterranean climate, the climate inland is moderately continental. This means that the winters can be cold inland — so much so that winter sports are perfectly possible.

The climate along the coast is mild throughout the winter. The only problem is the bora — a cold and very gusty wind that sometimes blows down from the mountains in the autumn and winter, mostly along the Croatian Coast, and which often causes the temperatures to plunge. There can also be a lot of rain in the winter, just as in other parts of the Mediterranean. On the other hand, the average winter temperatures along the coast are higher than those on the French and Italian Rivieras, which are a popular winter holiday destination.

The high season for tourists is July and August. This is also the hottest season, but the vegetation along the coast makes the climate more pleasant than it might otherwise be. Another pleasant feature is the maestral — a light, refreshing sea breeze that develops in the afternoons. The overall effect is ideal for getting brown in the sun. But it is not advisable to spend too long inland during the hottest months, as the climate there can become unpleasantly hot.

The bathing season begins as early as May or June, and goes on into September or October. The exact timing depends on both local and seasonal weather conditions, though one can generally expect the first autumn storms to begin soon after the beginning of October. But undoubtedly the best time to travel is in the mid-season (May/June or September/October).

It must also be borne in mind that the high season is also the main holiday period for native Yugoslavians, making the beaches along the coast even busier than ever. And even outside the main tourist areas, there are numerous holiday camps built by Yugoslavian companies for the benefit of their workers.

1 TOUR OF ISTRIA

From Ankaran to Opatija (about 200km)

The Istrian Peninsula takes its name from one of the Illyrian tribes called the Istri, which was conquered by the Romans in about 200 BC. In 178 BC the Romans founded the military colony of Pola (now Pula). In the seventh century AD the peninsula was settled by Croats and Slovenes, but it still remained part of the Byzantine Empire. It was conquered by Charlemagne, who absorbed it into the Frankish Empire. At the Treaty of Verdun in 843, it became part of the kingdom of Lothar I. The rulers changed frequently during subsequent centuries, though Venice gained an increasing control over the peninsula. In 1814 it became Austrian for more than a century. It came to Italy in 1919, but since 1947 it has been part of Yugoslavia.

Istria is a triangular-shaped peninsula lying between the Gulf of Trieste to the north and the Kvarner Gulf to the south-east. It has a total area of 5,000sq km, including numerous small offshore islands. The coastline is about 400km long, while the peninsula is roughly 50km wide at its base, measured along a line from Trieste to Rijeka. The main port is Pula*, though Rijeka* is only a short distance away along the Croatian Coast.

Though a geographical unit, the peninsula is politically and administratively divided. A small area in the north belongs to the constituent republic of Slovenia; this includes the towns of Koper and Portoroz. The rest belongs to Croatia. Opatija forms the centre of the so-called Kvarner Riviera at the northern end of the east coast of Istria.

Geologically speaking, Istria consists mostly of limestone, with a predominance of karst scenery (the word comes from the Karst or Krst region around Trieste). The west coast is fairly gentle, and is

41

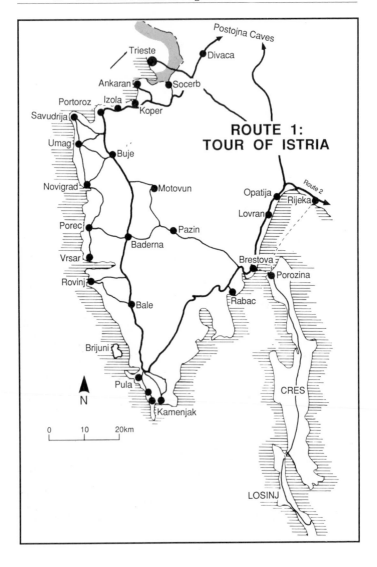

Piran, port on the Istrian Peninsula

even quite fertile in places. It is bordered by hills that form a beautiful
setting for the villages that crown them. The many offshore islets are

covered with pinewoods. The east coast is more mountainous, the highest point being the Ucka (1,368m (4,487ft)) overlooking the beach resort of Opatija. Across the Kvarner Gulf are the islands of Cres* and Losinj. The coasts are irregular, with long inlets such as the Limski Zaliv in the west and the Rasa and Plomin inlets to the east.

The dry soils mean that the vegetation tends to be sparse. But the more fertile valleys support trees such as willow, poplar and elm, and sometimes even oak and beech forests. The west coast is covered mostly with bushes, while the east coast tends to support ever-greens. The two main agricultural products are olives and wine, though fruit and vegetables are also grown. There is a small amount of livestock, while fishing is important in the towns and villages along the coast.

The Route

The most northerly settlement on the Yugoslav coast is the small resort of **Ankaran**. It lies across the bay from the town of Koper, from which it can be reached by bus or motorboat. It is 20km south of Trieste, and is reached via a turning off the main road about 3km north of Koper. The beach is rocky with pebbles, but is surrounded by pleasant green hills. A disused monastery has been turned into an extensive hotel complex.

Koper* (Capodistria) is 24km south of Trieste. A small port, it is full of historical interest. Though built on an island, it is linked to the coast by two causeways. Koper is 102km from Pula* (see below) near the southern end of the peninsula.

The next place along the coast is **Izola** (Isola), which is just below the main road about 7km west of Koper. This small town still has a few lovely old Venetian houses, including the fifteenth-century House of the Manzolis and the eighteenth-century Palazzo Be-senghi. The old cathedral is in a commanding position, with a good view along the coast to Trieste. Izola is well known for its bone-lace, its sardines and its wine. The Refosco is famous as a sweet dessert wine. The local fruit and vegetables are good, and especially the early strawberries. Just outside the town is a hotel complex with a small bathing beach and an indoor pool.

The next town along the main road is **Portoroz** (Portorose). It lies

The fascinating architecture of Koper

on the north shore of the Bay of Piran, together with the holiday suburb of Lucija. The surrounding hill slopes provide shelter from the cold north winds, favouring lush, subtropical vegetation (the Italian name Portorose means 'port of roses'). The salt springs nearby have encouraged its development as a health resort. Of particular interest is the so-called Forma Viva, an open-air sculpture museum on the Seca Peninsula. The holiday resort of Portoroz is internationally famous, thanks to its modern hotels, its beautiful beaches and coves (including a secluded nudist beach), and its wide choice of sporting and leisure activities.

The old Venetian port of **Piran** (Pirano) is perched on the headland beyond. The harbour on the south shore and the Tartini Square are surrounded by fine old Gothic and Baroque buildings. In the square is a statue of Tartini, the famous violinist, who was born in Piran. The town is dominated by the cathedral, which though begun in 1317 was not completed until 1637. It is topped by an enormous weathervane consisting of a bronze statue of St George. The medieval atmosphere is further enhanced by the old city walls, with their beautifully preserved battlements. Not far from the harbour are a nautical museum and an aquarium. There is a lighthouse

Umag, perched on the coastal headland

standing on the furthest point of the headland. The beach, though shingly, is quite suitable for bathing.

East of Piran and north of Portoroz is the tiny hamlet of **Fiesa**, which lies immediately above a beautiful little cove hidden by cliffs. It is a magical spot for bathing, with its clear blue waters, romantic setting and a small freshwater lake next to the beach. No more than a ridge separates it from the towns of Portoroz and Piran, making it an ideal place for visitors to escape to from the hustle and bustle.

The main road soon turns inland and continues south towards Pula via Buje and Baderna. But there is a coast road that turns right off the main road at Kaldanija, 11km from Portoroz. After 14km it arrives at the small fishing village and bathing resort of **Savudrija**. It is surrounded by extensive pine forests, and is the most westerly

Novigrad

point of the peninsula. An old lighthouse highlights the rocky character of the coastline. The pebble beach is suitable for non-swimmers,
and there are several children's holiday camps nearby. Four kilometres to the south are the partly submerged ruins of the Roman port
of Sipara.

The small town of **Umag** is perched on a headland about 8km
further down the coast. Umag is famous for its wine cellars, and the
old town is well worth a visit. Punta out on the headland has several
hotels and a casino. But the main tourist area is 3km to the north at
Katoro, where there are hotels and gardens lining the beach, and a
huge leisure centre with sporting facilities and a sea-water swimming
pool.

The coast road continues south through varied scenery, and after

Poreč, one of the most popular resorts in Istria

16km arrives at **Novigrad** (Cittanova d'Istria). This ancient town lies on a promontory to the north of the Mirna estuary, which is known as the Tarski Zaliv. The ruins of the former Roman port of Aemonia are still visible beneath the water. Further ancient remains are on display at the Palazzo Urizzi. The medieval cathedral contains an eighteenth-century altar; among the old sarcophagi in the late Romanesque crypt are the remains of St Pelagius. The pebble beach and the associated hotels are on a separate site from the old town.

There are link roads connecting Umag and Novigrad with the small inland town of **Buje** which is 17km south of Portoroz along the main road. The old Venetian town of Buje is delightfully situated on a hill (220m (722ft)). The sixteenth-century parish church and fifteenth-century church of Sveta Marija (St Mary) are of particular interest.

The inland parts of Istria are peppered with fascinating old hill-top settlements. Just off the main road to the south is the old fortified town of **Groznjan**, with its lovely Baroque church. Further inland is **Motovun** (Montona), where the original thirteenth-century walls were further strengthened between the fourteenth and seventeenth centuries. It also has an interesting sixteenth-century church.

Pazin (Pisino) is the main town in the centre of Istria. Its lovely medieval buildings include a Franciscan monastery; and there is a wonderful view from the old castle of Count Montecuccoli. The return route to Baderna on the main road passes through **Beram**, where the church contains some beautiful fifteenth-century frescos.

Baderna is 32km south of Buje along the main road. A link road leads back to **Porec*** (Parenzo) on the coast (12km), which is 15km south of Novigrad (see above). The small town of Porec is full of cultural and historical interest. It is one of the most popular tourist centres in the whole of Istria, and there are several holiday villages in the vicinity.

Ten kilometres further south, the coast road comes to an end at **Vrsar**. This pretty little fishing village has a lovely Romanesque church, and there is a hotel development nearby. The area is famous for its wines, and also for its quarries, which have provided stone for many beautiful buildings in Venice and Ravenna. There is a nudist colony on the offshore island of Koversada.

Immediately to the south of Vrsar is a narrow inlet called the

Limski Zaliv (Canale di Leme). It is 12km long, with cliffs up to 120m (394ft) high. The road from the coast to the main road (11km) runs close to its northern shore. At the far end, the main road passes close to an oyster farm. The restaurants immediately below the road serve oysters and other local delicacies. The nudist beach of Valalta on the south shore is accessible from Rovinj.

South of the inlet another side-road leads back down to the coast. After 13km it arrives at the beautiful little port of **Rovinj*** (Rovigno). Another road returns inland and rejoins the main road at the nice little Venetian town of **Bale**. The main road continues south to the delightful hill-top settlement of **Vodnjan** (11km), with its beautiful fifteenth-century houses. It is now only 10km to the busy port of **Pula*** (Pola), which is Istria's main cultural and administrative centre.

The route turns north-east towards Labin (42km) on the east coast of the peninsula. The road runs inland for a while, passing through the small medieval village of **Barban**. It crosses the Rasa, and runs close to the many-branched Rasa Inlet (Canale d'Arsa). It also passes through two coal-mining settlements called Rasa and Podlabin.

Labin (Albona) is perched high up on the mountainside. The narrow streets contain some lovely old fifteenth- and sixteenth- century houses. The church was also built in the sixteenth century. The highest point of the town is the castle, from which there is a marvellous view across the Kvarner Gulf to the islands beyond.

A small side-road drops down to the nearby seaside resort of **Rabac** (Porto Albona). Rabac is gorgeously situated in a steep-sided bay, surrounded by vineyards and subtropical vegetation. There are magnificent views along the Kvarner Riviera, and across the gulf to the island of Cres*. There is a hotel settlement nearby; the beach is fairly shallow and suitable for children.

Shortly before Plomin (14km from Labin) there is a turning along a road going inland towards Pazin and Banderna (see above). The old village of **Plomin** is perched above a long inlet called the Plominska Zaliv, whose waters are of a striking green colour. The road continues along the coast, with some breathtaking views of the mighty Ucka and the Kvarner Gulf. At one point it passes a motel perched precipitously on the cliffside. About 10km beyond Plomin,

Moscenicka Draga, near Opatija

there is a turning for **Brestova**, from which a ferry crosses this narrow part of the gulf to Porozina on the island of Cres*.

About 8km further on is the former fishing village of **Moscenicka Draga**. It is only 15km from Opatija, and forms the southern end of the magnificent Kvarner Riviera. The small pebble beach is quiet and suitable for children and non-swimmers. Further on, the coast becomes more rocky and the beach more stony. There are some lovely walks along the shore past private houses and villas.

About 180m (590ft) up the hillside, and just off the main coast road, the village of **Moscenice** still retains some of its old fortifications. It too provides some marvellous views. The next place is the small fishing village of **Medveja**, which also has a very good beach.

This is immediately followed by **Lovran**, which is like a small version of Opatija (see below), but is quieter and prettier. It too is protected by the Ucka from the cold north winds. Less cosmopolitan than Opatija, it nonetheless provides plenty of hotel accommodation. The beach is idyllic, and is surrounded by lush subtropical vegetation. A settlement is recorded here from as early as the ninth century,

Medveja

and there is evidence of earlier Roman remains. The old town has
retained many of its lovely old streets, and the Gothic church contains
frescos from the fifteenth century. There is an old tower dating back
to the twelfth century, and the small harbour completes the picture.

The next 10km stretch of coast has effectively become one long
holiday resort that has swallowed up the old villages of Ika and Icici.
Gardens, parks, villas and hotels follow one another in a single array.
A promenade runs along the shore, parallel to the main road, which
eventually enters the suburbs of Opatija.

Ancient streets, Lovran

Opatija (Abbazia) is the undisputed centre of the Kvarner Riviera, and one of the most popular of all Yugoslavian seaside resorts. Its name means 'abbey', and refers to a small fifteenth-century monastery that still stands in one of the parks. Opatija was no more than a small fishing village until 1844, when a citizen of Rijeka built a house and gardens here. The biggest growth occurred at the turn of the century, when a branch line was built from Rijeka. People flocked here from all over the Austro-Hungarian Empire. Although much has been modernised since then, the resort has retained its unmistakably Austrian character.

Opatija is still a famous international resort. Some of the modern hotels even have such luxuries as heated sea-water swimming pools. There is everything a tourist could wish for, from cafés and restaurants to cinemas and nightclubs. The open-air theatre stages concerts and folklore events, and there is dancing in front of the restaurants along the promenade; those on the terrace of the great Kvarner Hotel are a special attraction. Many great national and international events are held here, including conferences, regattas and car and motorbike races.

The central park is full of trees of all kinds: native oaks and chestnuts, agaves, bamboos, palms, cacti, magnolia, banana and lemon trees. Visitors may either use one of the three main beaches — Slatina, Opatija or Kvarner Lido — or else use the private beach in front of the hotel. There is a marvellous view across the gulf to the islands of Cres* and Krk*.

If one goes north-east from Opatija, whether along the coast road or along the road up to Matulji, there is a wonderful view back along the east coast of the Istrian Peninsula. **Veprinac** is also worth visiting. This lovely old village is perched on the mountainside at a height of 500m (1,640ft). The medieval church has been partly rebuilt in the Baroque style. More adventurous visitors may continue from here to the summit of the Ucka (1,368m (5,198ft)).

It is only 11km from Opatija to Rijeka*, which forms the starting point for the next part of the route.

2 THE CROATIAN COAST

From Rijeka to Karlobag (about 145km)

It is true that most of coastal Yugoslavia is inhabited by Croats, the only exceptions being the northern strip of Istria and the Montenegrin Coast in the south. It is also true that the same stretch of the coastline belongs to the constituent republic of Croatia. However, the Croatian Coast consists only of the northern part of the coast as far as the northern border of the former province of Dalmatia. The name Croatia (in Serbo-Croat Hrvatska) comes from the Slavic race that settled in the region in the seventh century AD.

The Croatian Coast extends from the city of Rijeka in the north to a short distance beyond the small town of Karlobag in the south. While the northern section is characterised by somewhat gentler slopes, the southern part is dominated by steep mountains that are almost bare of vegetation. In the north the coastal ranges are rarely above 1,000m (3,280ft), whereas south of Senj they are regularly over 1,500m (4,920ft).

The most popular tourist resorts are along the northern section of the coast, Crikvenica and Novi Vinodolski being the most popular of all. The mountain slopes come right down to the shore, but they are less steep than further south, and are covered with green vegetation. Further south the scenery is much more wild and dramatic. The Velebit Mountains rise almost vertically above the coastline, leaving precious little space for the tiny fishing villages that cling to the shores.

The regularity of the mountain ranges is reflected in the coastline, which has far fewer inlets than other parts of the coast. The only very large inlet is the Bay of Bakar, which is not far from Rijeka. Apart from the Vinodol region near Novi, the region is not particularly fertile. The

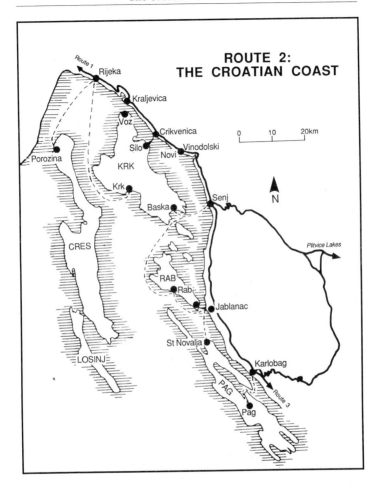

ROUTE 2:
THE CROATIAN COAST

people live mostly from fishing and agriculture. There is a considerable amount of industry around Rijeka in the north.

Rijeka is the starting point for the Adriatic Highway or Jadranska magistrala that runs all the way down the coast. This road is in an excellent state of repair throughout the Croatian section of the route. But there are relatively few link roads to the interior.

There are many islands off the coast here, both large and small.

From the mainland they look rocky and bare, but their western shores facing the sea are often greener and more fertile, with a substantial covering of trees. They are called the **Kvarner Islands**, and the largest of them are **Cres***, **Krk*** and **Rab***. Part of the island of **Pag*** also straddles this coast, but it more properly belongs to the Dalmatian Islands.

Most of the tourist centres on the islands, like those on the mainland, have large colonies of modern hotels in addition to the more modest older accommodation. The larger centres have good ferry links with Rijeka and other towns along the coast. There is also a wide choice of island excursions.

The Route

Rijeka* (Fiume) is Yugoslavia's largest port, and the main transit point for visitors to the islands along the Yugoslavian Coast. The main coast road leaves the city in a south-easterly direction via the suburb of Susak. It is 38km from Rijeka to Crikvenica.

After about 10km the road suddenly swings north-westwards, and loops around the Bay of Bakar. There is a viewing point with a glorious panorama of the bay, which is mostly surrounded by steep, inhospitable cliffs. It has recently been turned into a commercial harbour.

Four kilometres further on, there is a side-road leading down to the small town of **Bakar**, which clings precariously to the cliffs far below. Bakar is the seat of a naval academy. Its main attractions are the twelfth-century cathedral of Sveti Andrija (St Andrew) and the fifteenth-century Frankopan (Frangipani) castle. The so-called Turkish House has a typically overhanging first floor, and several other buildings have sixteenth-century inscriptions. There is a bathing beach among the nearby pinewoods, though recent industrialisation has made it somewhat unconducive to bathing. The local sparkling wine is very good; it is called Bakarska Vodica.

To the south-east at the entrance of the bay is the small fishing village of **Bakarac**, which also has a few vineyards nearby. The ladders that run out across the water are an indication that tunny fish (tuna) are caught here. When the coastguards see a school of tunny entering the bay, the fishermen lay their nets right across the entrance to bar their escape.

About 9km from Bakar is the small port of **Kraljevica**. It too lies well below the road, next to a small cove that faces north-westwards. The town was founded in the fifteenth century, and there are two seventeenth-century castles by the shore. The older one belonged to the Frankopans (Frangipani), and now has a bell tower attached. The other one was built by Count Zrinjski, and has a tower at each corner. The shipyard in the harbour was rebuilt following its destruction in World War II; it was then named after President Tito, who worked there in his youth. There is a beach at Ostro on the nearby headland, opposite the island of Sveti Marko.

Just to the south of Kraljevica is a modern bridge linking the island of Krk* with the mainland; it was built in 1980, and is 1.3km long. There are several turnings off the main road between here and Crikvenica; they lead down to the many beaches and holiday settlements that line the straits between the mainland and Krk. The first of these is Uvala Scott; closer to Crikvenica there are Dramalj and Kacjak. The beaches tend to be rocky or shingly.

Crikvenica is the best-known resort on the Croatian Coast. There is a ferry from here to Silo on the island of Krk*, which faces it across the strait. The coast is gently sloping and covered with forest, which makes it less hot in the summer. There is a good view of the town from the ruins of the old Frankopan castle. The long promenade is lined by an extensive sandy beach, which is rare for Yugoslavia. This resort is thus particularly well suited to children and to non-swimmers. There is also a modern health clinic, where sea-water therapy is practised.

Only 3km further on is the old fishing village of **Selce**, which is linked to Crikvenica by a promenade. Selce is developing rapidly as a holiday resort, with hotels and leisure facilities springing up in both directions.

Running parallel to the coast here is a famous valley called the **Vinodol**. Its name is very appropriate as it means 'wine valley'. It is about 25km long, and comes out onto the coast at Novi Vinodolski. This fertile valley is in stark contrast to the dry karst scenery of the area around.

Novi Vinodolski, often known simply as Novi, is one of the most beautifully situated towns on the Croatian Coast. The view from the harbour is particularly impressive, with the small town straddling the

Crikvenica

slopes above. The lovely fourteenth-century bell tower adds to the beauty of the scene. Overlooking the town are the remains of the old Frankopan castle, where the first Croatian law, the Vinodolski Statute, was passed in 1288.

The bathing beach and holiday village of **Lisanj** lies somewhat to the south-east of the town, but is linked to it via a promenade. Close by are the ruins of the Roman settlement of Lopari. The island of Krk* is still visible across the Vinodolski Kanal (or Vinodol Channel), which is much wider here than at Crikvenica. To the south is an island with a chapel called Sveti Marinus. There are two other hotel beaches near Novi: Zagori to the north and Povile to the south; both of them have good bathing facilities.

About 6km further on, the newly built coast road makes a wide loop around the Bay of Zrnovnica. The old road is still visible below; it is narrow and twisty as it climbs up and down around the hillside. The coast becomes increasingly steep and dramatic during the next 19km to Senj, with impressive views of Krk* across the Vinodolski Kanal.

The old town of **Senj*** lies huddled beneath the wild mountains of the Velebit. A road goes inland from here over the Vratnik Pass, leading eventually to the Plitvice Lakes* (72km). There are ferries from Senj to the islands of Krk* and Rab*.

The coast road continues south from Senj across the bare mountainside, often with a drop of some 200m (656ft) or 300m (984ft) down to the sea below. Tiny villages cling to the shore far below; first there is **Jurjevo**, then **Lukovo** and **Starigrad**. The views are naturally very impressive, both along the coast and across to the islands. Krk* is soon followed by the three small islands of Prvic, Sveti Grgur and Goli, and eventually by Rab*.

Forty kilometres south of Senj is the village of **Jablanac**, which is reached via a small side-road. It clings to the mountainside at the foot of the Velebit, in a small cove facing the southern tip of the island of Rab. There are ferries from here to Pudarica on Rab* and to Stara Novalja on the island of Pag*. A cable car runs 1,300m (4,264ft) up the side of a nearby peak called the Alan; it is used for transporting wood down the mountainside for shipment. Immediately to the south is the Zavratnica Fjord, where the sea forms a 2km-long breach in the mountainside; it can be reached via a path that has been partly hewn out of the cliff.

The coast road continues southwards across a mountainside that is bare of vegetation. The scenery is wild and impressive, with sheer cliffs dropping down into the sea. Soon the island of Pag* comes into view across the Velebitski Kanal; it is similarly bare and rocky.

Thirty kilometres from Jablanac the road arrives at **Karlobag**, which is the last place of any size before the Dalmatian border. The most interesting building is a Capuchin monastery with a library, and there is a ruined castle on the hillside above. There is a ferry from here to Pag(*) on the island of the same name.

At the eastern end of the village there is a turning along a steep, twisty road that climbs up over the **Stara Vrata Pass** (927m (3,040ft)). From the top there is a magnificent view of the coast and of the irregular-shaped island of Pag*. This road continues north-east in the direction of the Plitvice Lakes* (106km).

The coast road, meanwhile, continues south-eastwards along the scenic coastline. After 30km it crosses the Dalmatian border, and begins Route 3 tour (see below).

3 THE DALMATIAN COAST

From Starigrad-Paklenica to Gruda (about 470km)

The Dalmatian Coast runs from the old border with Croatia (just south of Karlobag opposite the island of Pag) to the Montenegrin border (just north of the Gulf of Kotor). For the purposes of this guide it has been divided into three sections. Of the 1,000 Yugoslavian islands, 800 are off the Dalmatian Coast.

Dalmatia was named after an Illyrian tribe called the Dalmati that lived along this part of the coast. The Greeks founded several colonies along the coast between the seventh and fourth centuries BC. The Romans eventually gained ascendency after a 200-year-long struggle. With the division of their empire in AD 395, Dalmatia became part of the Western Empire. In the seventh century it became part of Croatia, which was later taken over by Hungary.

From AD 1000 onwards the Venetians began to colonise the coast, and by the fifteenth century had nearly all of it under their control. The advancing Turks never managed to remove them, and Dalmatia remained Venetian until Venice eventually fell to Austria. The only city to remain independent was Ragusa (Dubrovnik).

The people living along the coast all speak Serbo-Croat; but they have nonetheless been greatly influenced by their former Venetian rulers, both culturally and to a small extent linguistically. Nowadays Dalmatia belongs to the constituent republic of Croatia.

3a The Northern Section

From Starigrad-Paklenica to Rogoznica (about 170km)

The two main towns in northern Dalmatia are Zadar* and Sibenik*. Apart from the mighty Velebit in the north, and the much gentler mountain ranges to the south, the hinterland is mostly hilly in character. There are some very interesting places to visit in a region which is remarkably fertile. The people live mostly from agriculture and wine production. On the coast there is also fishing, and a small amount of shipbuilding in the larger ports. In general, however, industry is developing fast.

The many islands off the coast form the northern part of the Dalmatian Islands*. The largest of these is Pag*, followed by Dugi Otok. The Kornat Archipelago is particularly interesting, with its numerous small islands and rocks.

The Route

About 30km south of Karlobag, the road crosses the former Dalmatian frontier between the two small villages of Lukovo and Tribanj. It is another 17km to **Starigrad-Paklenica** which is built on the site of the Roman city of Argurunturum. The most interesting features are the twelfth-century church and the remains of the medieval fortifications. There is a large hotel and a nudist beach.

The surrounding area is particularly beautiful. Nearby is the fascinating **Paklenica National Park** — a karst region of cliffs, gorges and caves that spreads out below the Vaganj (1,785m (5,855ft)), the highest peak of the Velebit. Of particular interest is the **Manita Pec** — a 500m-long (1,640ft) complex of caverns lying at 580m (1,902ft) above sea level. A kilometre along the main road from Starigrad, there is a marvellous view along the **Paklenica Gorge**, with the summit of the Vaganj beyond.

Fourteen kilometres further on, and just before Maslenica, there is a left turn for **Obrovac** which is famous for its costumes. Shortly before Obrovac, there is another turning along a small side-road over the **Mali Alan Pass** (1,045m (3,427ft)), from which there are magnificent views. Immediately above Obrovac itself, there is a view along the gorge of the Zrmanja, which is navigable as far as Obrovac.

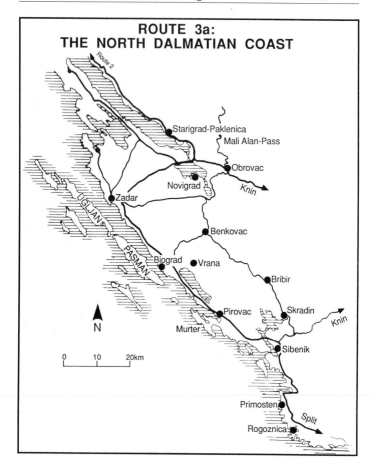

ROUTE 3a:
THE NORTH DALMATIAN COAST

Paklenica, a karst region of cliffs, gorges and caves

Obrovac is prettily situated at the foot of a steep hill with a ruined thirteenth-century castle.

At **Maslenica** (32km from Zadar) the main coast road crosses a long bridge over the Novigradsko Zdrilo (Novigrad Channel), which links the Novigradsko More (Novigrad Sea) with the sea. About 5km after the bridge there is a right turn along a side-road leading to the island of Pag*. A short way beyond this is the village of **Posedarje**, which is surrounded by vineyards and olive groves.

A left turn at Posedarje brings one along the southern shore of the Novigrad Sea to the small fishing port of **Novigrad**. Novigrad is famous for its mussels and its lovely old Croatian parish church. It too is overlooked by a ruined thirteenth-century castle. The road carries on eastwards to **Karin**, and eventually arrives at a fifteenth-century Franciscan monastery by the Karinsko More (Karin Sea); this is also accessible from Obrovac and Zadar* (see page 197).

The main road continues from Posedarje through the fertile region where the marasca cherry is grown. It is another 24km to **Zadar*** (Zara), the one-time capital of Dalmatia. Zadar is an ideal base from which to visit the Dalmatian Islands* and the fascinating north Dalmatian hinterland. There are ferries to many of the islands, and also across the Adriatic Sea to Ancona in Italy.

During the next section to Sibenik (73km), the main road runs along the coast opposite the islands of Ugljan and Pasman. It passes through several lovely little seaside resorts. **Bibinje** is situated on a small peninsula; **Sukosan** (10km from Zadar) lies by a beautiful bay; and the pebble beach at **Filip-Jakov** (another 15km) is surrounded by pinewoods.

Biograd* (another 5km) is a popular seaside resort, with some fascinating places to visit nearby. There is a ferry service to Tkon, which lies across the channel on the island of Pasman (see the Dalmatian Islands*).

Just to the south of Biograd is the peaceful holiday village of **Crvena Luka**, which offers marvellous facilities for bathing and watersports. A short way further on there is another turning for **Pakostane** (6km from Biograd) — a pretty fishing village surrounded by olive groves, vineyards and pinewoods that line the shore. The holiday complex nearby belongs to the French tourist organisation Club Méditerranée.

Only a short distance inland is Dalmatia's largest inland lake, the **Vransko Jezero**. It is 14km long with a maximum width of 4km, and is a popular place for hunting feathered game. It is named after the small village of **Vrana**, which is 6km from the main road along a small turning that turns off just before Pakostane. Nearby are the remains of a monastery built by the Knights Templar in the twelfth century.

The coast road continues southwards along the narrow strip of land that divides the Vransko Jezero from the sea. There are some marvellous views of the offshore islands. It is another 15km to the seaside resort of **Pirovac** which is pleasantly situated next to a wide bay. It provides plentiful accommodation and bathing facilities (including a nudist beach).

Four kilometres further on there is a turning for the island of Murter (see the Dalmatian Islands*), which is linked by a swingbridge to the mainland. A good 10km from Pirovac is the delightful little fishing port and market town of **Vodice**. It has a bathing beach with a promenade and good hotel accommodation. Proseko wines are produced in this area.

The Kornat Archipelago

The village of Primosten

Seven kilometres beyond Vodice the coast road crosses a long viaduct over the wide channel formed by the lower reaches of the Krka; there are impressive views in either direction. It is now only another 6km to the port of **Sibenik*** (Sebenico). The fascinating old parts of the town are now bypassed by the main road. Visitors are especially recommended to visit the beautiful **Krka Falls** near Skradin (15km), and to take a boat trip around the nearby **Kornat Archipelago** (see the Dalmatian Islands*).

The main road continues along the beautiful coastline. There are a few more islands, such as Krapanj (about 7km from Sibenik), but the views after that are mostly across the open sea. Twenty-eight kilometres south of Sibenik there is a right turn leading down to the delightful little village of **Primosten**. It was built on a small island that is linked to the mainland by a causeway. Hotels have sprung up along the headland opposite.

Six kilometres further along the main road, there is a right turn leading down to **Rogoznica** which like Primosten is situated on an island linked to the mainland by a causeway. There are some beautiful beaches along the bays either side of the village.

3b The Central Section

Rogoznica to Opuzen (about 180km)

The central section of the Dalmatian Coast extends from Rogoznica in the north to the mouth of the Neretva in the south. The coast runs eastwards for a short distance, but after Split it turns south-east again. The vegetation is noticeably lusher than further north, and the more mountainous terrain makes the scenery much more dramatic than in the area around Zadar. The rugged peaks of the Mosor and Biokovo ranges are particularly impressive.

Split* is the main cultural and economic centre of the region. West of Split is the beautiful medieval town of Trogir* — and between them the famous Kastelanski Riviera, with its seven castles, and the ancient Roman city of Salona. The chief seaside resorts in this important holiday region include Brela, Makarska*, Tucepi and Podgora.

The islands off this part of the coast are somewhat larger than those further north. They also have more vegetation, and some of them are positively subtropical in character. The trees in particular help to moderate the heat in the summer. Hvar* is particularly favoured climatically, and is correspondingly popular as a holiday destination.

The Route

The first place after Rogoznica is **Marina**, which lies just off the main road on a north-facing slope. Its most interesting feature is a square tower next to the shore. The sea here forms a long inlet running parallel to the coast.

Twelve kilometres further on is the small town of **Trogir*** (Traù), which again lies just off the main road. It is situated on a small island in the channel that runs between the mainland and the island of Ciovo (see the Dalmatian Islands*), and is linked to both of them via bridges. This lovely little town has so beautifully retained its medieval character that it is almost a museum in itself.

It is 28km from Trogir to Split along the modern road, but travellers are recommended to use the old road; this runs closer to the shore along the famous **Kastelanski Riviera** or Bay of Seven Castles.

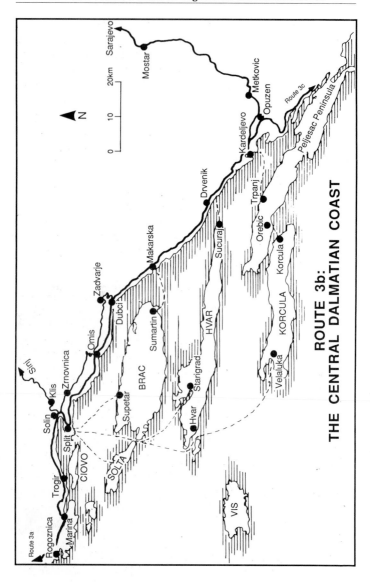

ROUTE 3b:
THE CENTRAL DALMATIAN COAST

These seven ruined forts are all that remain of the original thirteen  that were built in the fifteenth century to repel the Turks. Each fort has a village built around it. The villages are called Kastel Stafilic, Kastel Novi, Kastel Stari, Kastel Luksic, Kastel Kambelovac, Kastel Gomilica and Kastel Sucurac. They have grown together with the development of modern tourism, and provide good accommodation and bathing facilities. The coastline is protected from the bora by the Kozjak mountain barrier. The result is a rich profusion of vines, fruit trees, olives and laurels, aloe, myrtle, pomegranates and almonds. The local wines are also famous.

The next place of interest is **Solin*** on the site of the former Roman city of Salona. Six kilometres beyond Solin is the city of **Split*** (Spalato), which is the main economic and cultural centre of Dalmatia. A road goes inland from here via Klis to Sinj, both of them worth a special excursion. There are numerous boat and ferry connections with offshore islands such as Brac*, Hvar*, Korcula*, Solta and Vis

Aerial view of Trogir, a 'museum town'

(see the Dalmatian Islands*).

At **Stobrec**, 8km east of Split, the coast road enters the former territory of the so-called Peasants' Republic or Free State of Poljica. It covered an area of 250sq km, including the coast between Stobrec and Omis (see below), plus a small area of the Mosor Mountains behind. This tiny state retained its independence from the twelfth century right up to the French occupation in 1807.

Sveti Petar chapel, Omis

Cetina

One can turn left off the main road at Stobrec and make a short scenic detour through the hinterland via Zrnovnica and **Gata**, which was the capital of the former republic. Gata lies directly above Omis, and the road down the hillside from Gata to Omis goes through some particularly dramatic scenery.

Omis (Almissa) is 18km along the coast from Stobrec. A former pirate settlement, it is in a beautifully dramatic setting at the mouth of the Cetina, which plunges through a rocky ravine on its way to the sea. In spite of the rocky terrain, there is a sandy beach at the end of the spit on which the town is built (sandy beaches are rare in Yugoslavia). Unfortunately Omis is also industrial. The people are mostly employed in industry, though some work in wine production (the local Proseko wines are famous).

Perched high on the rock behind the town are the ruins of the former pirate fortress of Mirabela. The old tenth-century Croatian chapel of Sveti Petar stands on the right bank of the Cetina; it has an unusual dome. The remains of the old town fortifications are still visible down by the harbour, where there is also a Franciscan monastery. The seventeenth-century church of Sveti Mihovil is remarkable for its beautiful west door. The pinewoods to the south-east of the town are the site for a modern hotel settlement (the beach is rocky with pebbles).

A short detour is recommended to visit the **Cetina Falls**. The Mala Gubavica is 7km from Omis along the road to Zadvarje. The Velika Gubavica is 13km further on, and plunges down the mountain-

The Makarska Riviera

side above the village of **Zadvarje**, which is also overlooked by a ruined castle. Another road leads back from Zadvarje back to the coast road at Dubci (9km).

The coast road meanwhile continues via the modern hotel settlement of **Ruskamen** (6km), where there is a beach with rocks and pebbles, to **Dubci** (another 11km), where the road comes in from Zadvarje (see above).

Six kilometres beyond Dubci the road arrives at **Brela** which has developed into a thriving resort. The old village clings to the hillside above, while the modern hotels spread out along the shore. The surrounding pinewoods create a particularly beautiful setting. The beach is again rocky with pebbles, but this at least means that the water is clear.

Only 2km from Brela is the tiny resort of **Baska Voda** which like

Beach and hotel at Tucepi

Brela is surrounded by pinewoods. There is a shore path running between the two resorts. The visitor is invariably struck by the sharp contrast between the lush greenery along the shore and the bare rocky landscape of the mountains behind.

There are two viewing points along the next part of the route, with views of the islands of Brac* and Hvar*. It is 10km to **Makarska***, the most popular of the resorts along this part of the coast, which is appropriately known as the Makarska Riviera (63km from Split). There is a ferry service from Makarska to Sumartin on the island of Brac*.

Tucepi is only 3km south of Makarska along the scenic coast road, and is well known as the site of the famous Jadran Hotel. The old village clings to the hillside above the shore. Of particular interest are the cemetery, with its *stecak* stones (Bogomil gravestones), and the church of Sveti Juraj, built in the thirteenth and fourteenth centuries. A side-road leads down from the village to a 2km-long beach, next to which is the modern beach resort of Tucepi Kraj. Tucepi is typical of the Makarska Riviera in being surrounded by green woodlands. The park next to the Jadran Hotel provides a rich display of lush Mediterranean flora.

Between Tucepi and Podgora (4km) there is a left turn along a road that climbs up over the Staza Pass (897m (2,942ft)). Visitors are recommended to make a short detour as far as the top of the pass. There are some magnificent views, both from points on the way up and from the summit.

Podgora is situated among olive groves at the foot of the mighty Biokovo Mountains. The village clings to the coast road, forming a swathe across the mountainside. A large war memorial commemorates the freedom struggles of the Yugoslav peoples. Podgora is famous as the birthplace of the Yugoslav navy during World War II. A side-road leads down to the beach, which is lined by modern hotels. There is a long line of small bays with beaches along the coast. Another small road runs back along the shore to Tucepi Kraj.

During the next 33km to Gradac, the coast road passes a number of lovely little villages. **Igrane** is situated off the road and down towards the shore; the bell tower on the church is particularly impressive. Then there is the monastery of Sivo Grozdje near **Zivogosce**, now a modern hotel resort surrounded by lush vegeta-

Podgora lies at the foot of the mighty Biokovo mountains

tion. From **Drvenik** there are ferry services to Sucuraj on the island of Hvar* and Trpanj on the Peljesac Peninsula*.

Zaostrog is surrounded by olive groves, and has a sixteenth-century monastery where the poet Kacic-Miosic was buried. **Gradac** is a fishing village at the foot of the Biokovo, but has developed into a pleasant holiday resort, with an extensive beach and well kept parks full of palm trees.

The main coast road turns inland, and continues through a karst landscape past several small lakes. After 15km there is a right turn for **Kardeljevo**. Formerly called Ploce, the town is situated by a bay. During recent years a major commercial port has developed here, which mostly handles timber and metal ores from the Bosnian hinterland. There are ferry services to Korcula(*) on the island of the same name, and to Trpanj on the long peninsula of Peljesac*. Kardeljevo is served by a narrow gauge railway, with passenger services to Metkovic (26km; see below), to the oriental-looking town of Mostar* (another 48km), and eventually to Sarajevo* (another 140km).

The main road enters the fascinating region of the **Neretva Delta**. Once an area of swamp, it has now been largely drained for farmland. It is criss-crossed by canals, which the local farmers use to get to their fields; they travel in barges or punts. The remaining marshes are famous for the rich variety of bird species that feed there, while the shallow waters are a paradise for anglers.

Travellers are recommended to make a short detour via Metkovic, turning off the main coast road along the north-west bank of the Neretva. Just off this road, near the tiny village of Vid, are the ruins of the former Roman settlement of **Narona**.

Metkovic is prettily situated on a slope overlooking the Neretva. Although 20km inland, it has a small harbour to which ships come up-river from the coast. There is an interesting ornithological collection, including local marshland birds. The Hutovo Blata to the east is an area of impenetrable swamp. South-west of Metkovic, near the hamlet of Kula Novinska, there are the remains of a Turkish fortress.

The main road runs closer to the coast, and crosses the Neretva at Rogotin (soon after Kardeljevo). It meets the road coming down from Metkovic near the village of **Opuzen** on the banks of the Neretva (about 7km upstream). The main attraction here is a seven-teenth-century Venetian tower.

The main road turns back towards the coast as it begins the next stage of the route.

3c The Southern Section

Opuzen to Gruda (about 120km)

The final section of the Dalmatian Coast runs from the Neretva Delta to the northern end of the Gulf of Kotor. The most southerly resort along this section of the coast is Cavtat, while the most northerly is Orebic on the Peljesac Peninsula*. Peljesac is linked to the mainland at Ston, and is the longest peninsula on the Dalmatian Coast. Its scenery is wild and rugged; the roads are steep and twisty, and often make for difficult driving.

The mainland coastline is similarly mountainous, though less so than the areas bordering the Biokovo range further north. The islands off the coast are smaller and fewer in number, and the only one of any significance is Lopud (see the Dalmatian Islands*). The islands seem almost visibly to dwindle as one travels down the coast.

Dubrovnik* is the most important town in every respect. Most of the seaside resorts cluster along the coast in both directions. All of them are surrounded by lush subtropical vegetation, which also helps to moderate the climate. The mountains by contrast are relatively bare of vegetation.

The people live mostly from agriculture and fishing, and to an increasing extent from tourism. There are fewer industrial plants than further north along the coast.

The Route

It is about 90km from the Neretva Delta to Dubrovnik. About 16km from Opuzen, the road passes through the small village of **Klek**, which is prettily situated opposite the Klek Peninsula. It is closely followed (after 4km) by the village of **Neum**, which is in a similarly beautiful setting. The restaurant above the camping site affords a marvellous panorama of the Peljesac Peninsula*.

Sixteen kilometres further on, and just before Dunta Doli, there is a right turn for Ston; this is the only overland route onto the **Peljesac Peninsula***.

It is another 14km to **Slano** which lies just off the main road at the end of a long inlet. Like other places along this part of the coast, Slano ónce belonged to the former Republic of Ragusa (Dubrovnik). The

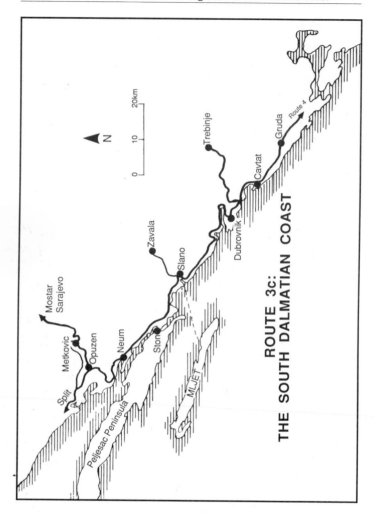

ROUTE 3c:
THE SOUTH DALMATIAN COAST

The Mestrovic Mausoleum, Cavtat

Cavtat

fourteenth-century Franciscan monastery contains the tombs of Bosnian noblemen. The former governor's palace dates back to the fifteenth century. Slano is famous for its annual market, held on 2 August every year. There is a shallow beach, and a ferry service to the island of Mljet (see the Dalmatian Islands*).

Cavers are recommended to make a short excursion inland to the great Vjetrenica Grotto near Zavala. The distance is only 15km, but the road is not very good. One can also make a small detour between Slano and Trsteno (13km) via the village of **Gornji Majkovi**. The road out of the village climbs to 370m (1,213ft), affording a magnificent view of the coast and the islands out to sea.

Trsteno is even smaller than Slano, and clings to the hillside

Dubrovnik

above the shore. It is a favourite destination for holidaymakers staying at Dubrovnik. The village square next to the church contains two 600-year-old plane trees with enormous trunks and tall crowns. They are two of the oldest plane trees in Europe. Not far away is the villa of Count Gozze-Gucetic, a noble family from Dubrovnik. The park adjoining it was first laid out in the sixteenth century, and has since been turned into a remarkable botanic garden. There are palms, cacti, oranges, laurels, cedars, cypresses, carob trees, pepper shrubs, judas trees and camphor trees. Finally, there is an 800-year-old oak tree standing next to a small chapel.

It is another 26km to Dubrovnik. The main road winds around the coast through some beautiful scenery, forming wide loops round the

Zaton and Dubrovacka inlets. The latter is formed by the Ombla or Rijeka Dubrovacka — an underground river which emerges from a 400m-high (1,312ft) cliff and runs for a further 5km before entering the Adriatic.

On its northern shore are the villages of **Mokosica**, with its iodine and sulphur baths, and **Rozat**, with its twelfth-century monastery. On the southern shore is the industrial village of **Komolac**, from which one can take a short cut to Dubac, bypassing the mountainous peninsula on which Dubrovnik lies.

The main coast road meanwhile follows the southern shore of the Dubrovacka from Komolac to the port of **Gruz** (Gravosa), then crosses the peninsula to the world-famous international tourist centre of **Dubrovnik*** (Ragusa). Anyone staying here is especially recommended to visit Trebinje, which is about 31km inland. There is also a ferry service across the Adriatic to Bari in Italy.

The main coast road continues southwards through some glorious scenery. It runs along the hillside above a series of small seaside resorts. The first is **Kupari**; once a centre for tile manufacture, it now boasts a good pebble beach. It is followed by **Srebreno** in the next bay. The coast is covered with lush vegetation, and it is easy to see why so many holiday villas have sprung up here. The road crosses the end of the Breno Valley or Dubrovacka Zupa, where considerable quantities of wine are produced.

The next resort is **Mlini**, which is surrounded by pinewoods, cypresses and olive groves. The beach is shallow and thus highly suitable for non-swimmers. Then there is **Plat** — a colony of hotels with pavilions overlooking a beautiful beach.

A small side-road leads off to **Cavtat** one of the finest resorts along the whole of the Yugoslavian coast. It is 19km from Dubrovnik, is surrounded by vineyards, and has gardens full of lemon and orange trees. There are ample bathing facilities, including the beaches along the Tiha Bay, the large heated sea-water pool, and private hotel pools.

Cavtat is built on the site of the former Graeco-Roman town of Epidaurus. Its inhabitants were forced to flee the Avars in the seventh century AD, and moved on to found the city of Ragusa (Dubrovnik). But a new settlement eventually grew up here. The birthplace of Bogisic, the famous lawyer and historian, contains his library and a museum of Roman antiquities. The birthplace of the Croat painter Bukovac has been turned into an art gallery. There is a beautifully laid-out cemetery on a hill overlooking the village, with a magnificent view of the sea and the mountains along the coast. A mausoleum was built here for the famous Racic family; it was created by Mestrovic in the 1920s.

Dubrovnik airport is another 5km south-east of Cavtat between Mocici and Cilipi. **Cilipi** is a good place for seeing national costumes on market day. It is situated in the fertile Konavlije Valley, which is so famous for its costumes. It is another 9km to **Gruda**, the main village in the valley. Soon after Gruda the road crosses the border into Montenegro.

4 THE MONTENEGRIN COAST

From Igalo to Ulcinj (about 150km)

T he Montenegrin Coast extends from Igalo on the Bay of Kotor to Sveti Nikola on the Albanian border. Montenegro is the smallest of the Yugoslavian constituent republics. The name is Venetian meaning 'black mountain', which is also the meaning of the republic's Serbo-Croat name Crna Gora.

The coast here is practically bereft of islands, but is nonetheless one of the most scenic parts of the whole coastline. The Gulf of Kotor is particularly beautiful, while the seaside resorts between Budva and Ulcinj provide sandy beaches in attractive surroundings.

The mountains near the coast reach a maximum height of 1,895m (6,215ft) in the Orjen range. The main ranges further south are the Lovcen (1,749m (5,737ft)) and the Rumija (1,593m (5,225ft)). The peaks are often bare and rugged, forming a delightful contrast to the lush greenery along the coast.

In the early spring of 1979, Montenegro was shaken by a severe earthquake. The landscape remained unaffected, but considerable damage was inflicted on the beautiful old towns of Kotor, Budva, Bar and Ulcinj. Most of the hotels have since been fully repaired.

The Route

The first part of the coast road is not particularly promising as it leaves the greenery of the Konavlije Valley for the more arid scenery of the Sutorina Valley. During the period of Turkish occupation, this valley formed the main corridor between Bosnia–Hercegovina and the sea. It now forms the boundary between Roman script (Croat) to the west and Cyrillic script (Serb) to the north and east (see page 218).

The seaside and spa resort of **Igalo** is 18km beyond Gruda.

The Gulf of Kotor

Though small, it has an extensive beach next to the Bay of Topla, which forms the first part of the Gulf of Kotor. The next village is **Topla** itself, which also has an excellent beach.

Topla is immediately followed by the little town of **Hercegnovi** (Castelnuovo), which is built in terraces on the hillside overlooking the shore. It is surrounded by lush vegetation, and the climate is unusually mild, making it an ideal winter resort. The north-eastern slopes of the nearby Orjen (1,895m) (6,215ft) provide skiing well into the spring, when it is already possible to bathe in the sea.

The town was founded in 1382 by King Tvrtko I of Bosnia. In 1483 it was captured by the Turks, and subsequently passed through the hands of the Spaniards, the Venetians, the Russians, the French and the Austrians. Many traces still remain of the town's unsettled past.

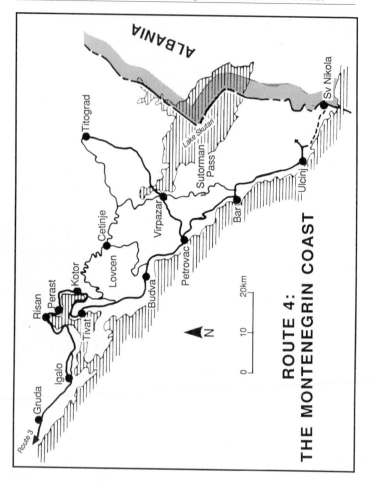

ROUTE 4:
THE MONTENEGRIN COAST

Items of interest include the bell tower and the Karadza Fountain in the main central square. Overlooking the town is the old Spanish fortress, Tvrdjava Spanjola, built in 1538. There are still some remains of the old Turkish and Venetian forts. The church of St Hieronimus contains an impressive painting of the saint himself together with the Virgin Mary. The park adjoining the Boka Hotel is planted with twenty different species of palm, and also provides some good views.

Two kilometres further on at **Savina** there is an eleventh-century Eastern Orthodox monastery. The smaller medieval church contains some lovely old frescos. The larger church was built in the eighteenth century; it includes a wall covered in icons and an extensive treasury. The monastery library also contains some valuable treasures.

It is another 45km to Kotor if one follows the road. Four kilometres beyond Hercegnovi is the small but lively port of **Zelenika**. Seven kilometres further on, the church at **Bijela** contains some valuable fourteenth-century frescos.

The road runs alongside the Kumbor Channel, which links the Bay of Topla with the Bay of Tivat, the second part of the Gulf of Kotor. The shore opposite belongs to the **Lustica Peninsula**, which is linked to the eastern side of the bay. There are boat trips to it from Hercegnovi, the most interesting feature being the Blue Grotto or Karadzunica, which is similar to the Blue Grotto on Capri.

The road carries on along the shore past several holiday beaches. Eleven kilometres east of Zelenika is the ferry port of **Kamenari**, from which a car ferry crosses the bay to Lepetane (see page 93). This is a good short-cut for cars travelling direct to Budva. The bay forms another channel here; the so-called Verige Kanal or Channel of Chains is only 300m (984ft) wide, and only just allows seagoing vessels to pass. Its name comes from the chains which were thrown across it as a defence during the Middle Ages. Beyond it is the Bay of Risan, the third part of the Gulf of Kotor.

The road follows the irregular shoreline to the small town of **Risan**, which is the oldest settlement in the region. It was first settled by Illyrians as early as the fifth century BC. It is overlooked by the two Turkish fortresses of Grkavac and Ledenica. The treasury in the sixteenth-century church of Sveti Petar i Pavle (St Peter and St Paul) contains a valuable Roman mosaic. The municipal park contains

The medieval town of Kotor

some other interesting remains. The people wear colourful local costumes at religious festivals. There is a small beach for tourists, and a certain amount of modest accommodation.

A side-road climbs up the hillside into the mountainous Krivosije region. Further along the shore towards Perast is the Banja Monastery. Originally built in the twelfth century, it was rebuilt in 1722.

It is another 4km to **Perast**, which is beautifully situated on the shore opposite the northern end of the Verige Channel. On the hillside above are the ruins of an old Venetian castle. Though Perast is now only a village, the extensive remains of old houses, palaces and churches bear witness to its glorious past.

In its heyday in the seventeenth and eighteenth centuries, there were some 3,000 people living here. It was the main commercial centre for the people of the bay, most of whom worked in the service of Venice. In the sixteenth century there was a naval academy here, where young Russian officers trained under Peter the Great. When

Secluded beach, Budva

steamers replaced sailing ships, the town soon dwindled into insignificance. The palaces decayed, and Perast gradually fell into ruin. Only now have they begun to restore some of the old buildings.

The seventeenth-century Baroque church was never completed. It has a fine bell tower and a rich collection of paintings and other treasures. The most impressive Baroque structure is the Bujovic Palace at the western end of the old town. It contains an interesting collection of exhibits from the past. The building of the former naval academy has been turned into a museum of oceanography.

There are two small islands out in the bay. The first of these is **Sveti Djordje** or **Sveti Juraj**, where there are the remains of a Benedictine abbey, destroyed by an earthquake in 1667. The island is in a highly romantic setting, and is supposed to have provided Arnold Böcklin with the inspiration for his painting *Isle of the Dead*.

Budva church

But there are other contenders for this title, including Punta San Vigilio in Lake Garda and the Greek island of Corfu.

The other island is called **Gospa od Skrpjela**. Originally no more than a reef, it was enlarged by the sinking of pirate vessels filled with stones. The church was built in 1628, and has since become a place of pilgrimage. On 15 August every year there is a seaborne procession to the island. The high altar inside the church is made of white marble from Genoa. The altarpiece above it dates back to the fourteenth century. The church is decorated with numerous paintings and votive offerings.

The road continues along the shore of the bay to the end of an inlet (15km), where the medieval town of **Kotor*** (Cattaro) nestles below the mighty Lovcen (1,759m (5,769ft)).

Visitors to Kotor are recommended to make an excursion to **Cetinje*** (41km). The route goes left up the Trojica Pass (231m (757ft)), then left again at the top of the pass. It skirts the great Lovcen massif and climbs over Bukovica Pass (1,247m (4,090ft)) before dropping down steeply into the former Montenegrin capital. The trip is highly recommended, both for the glorious scenery on the way and for the buildings in the old town itself.

The main road meanwhile follows the shore of the bay from Kotor in the direction of Lepetane. The first village is **Prcanj** (5km), which clings to the eastern slopes of the Vrmac (750m (2,460ft)). The lovely Renaissance parish church was begun in 1789, but was not finished until the present century; it contains some valuable treasures. Like other villages on the bay Prcanj retains a number of old buildings from its former seafaring days. The beach is shallow and ideal for bathing.

At **Lepetane** the road meets the ferry from Kamenari across the Channel of Chains (see page 89). It continues around the coast to **Tivat**. Tivat clings to the shore of the Bay of Tivat beneath the western slopes of the Vrmac. There is a good beach and a large park filled with exotic plants. The town is an old one, with a fine old fourteenth-century church. But it has recently been rather spoilt by modern industrial developments, including a small shipyard. The airport to the south is only used during the summer season.

There are several small islands out in the bay to the south: on **Sveti Marko** there is a camping site and a Club Méditerranée holiday camp; on **Prevlaka** there is yet another ruined abbey.

The coast road from Tivat crosses the neck of land adjoining the Lustica Peninsula. After 24km it comes out by the sea again at **Budva**. There was a Greek colony on this site as early as the fourth century BC; the Romans called it Butua, and it was one of the oldest

Sveti Stefan

settlements on the coast of Montenegro.

The small town is delightfully situated on a small promontory, surrounded by its old medieval walls. It was unfortunately badly damaged in the earthquake of 1979, and the same is true of the hotels in the nearby holiday villages of Mogren and Slovenski Plaza. By 1989 everything should be back in its original state. A new hotel complex is also being built along the coast.

Two excursions are recommended from Budva: a boat trip to Sveti Nikola, a small, rocky island off the coast; and a trip inland through beautiful mountain scenery to the former Montenegrin capital of Cetinje* (33km). The road to Cetinje leaves the coast road about 3km along the shore.

About 1km beyond this turning is the holiday village of **Becici**, which still belongs to Budva and has a good extensive beach. Four kilometres along the bay, the village of **Milocer** is surrounded by lush vegetation. The park adjoining it contains the former royal summer residence, which has now been turned into a hotel. The Hotel Maestral is a kilometre away, but is considerably more modern.

A short way further on, the old village of **Sveti Stefan** is perched on a rock that is linked to the mainland by a narrow sandbar. This medieval fortified town has become a major tourist attraction, and all the houses have been converted into hotel apartments. However, great care was taken to preserve their original exteriors. Nearby is the medieval Orthodox monastery of **Praskvica**, which contains some beautiful frescos.

The road continues along the coast, with some magnificent views in both directions. After 9km it bends sharply to the left so that one can look right down on **Petrovac**. The village clings to the shore of a bay, surrounded by slopes covered in vineyards, olive groves and pine-woods. The bathing is good, and there are the remains of some Roman mosaics. At the other end of the village is an old fortress called Kastel Lasstva. Other places of interest are the nearby monasteries of **Gradiste** and **Rezevic**, which contain some fine frescos. Two small rocky islands off the shore are each crowned by a church; they are called Sveta Nedelja and Katic.

At Petrovac the coast road forms a junction with the main road to Titograd. This road goes inland over a pass (700m (2,296ft)) and drops down to the lovely little town of **Virpazar** (27km) by **Lake**

Scutari. Known in Serbo-Croat as the **Skadarsko Jezero**, it is the biggest inland lake in the Balkans. It is 48km long by 14km wide, and straddles the Albanian border. The Albanian shores are flat and marshy, while the south-western shores on the Yugoslavian side are overlooked by the mighty Rumija Mountains. Originally an inlet of the sea, it was dammed back by silt coming down from the mountains. It is full of fish, which provide food for large flocks of water birds such as pelicans. The shores are lined with a thick carpet of water lilies and other aquatic plants.

The road continues across an arm of the lake, and carries on inland towards the Montenegrin capital of Titograd* (30km).

The coast road meanwhile continues south-east from Petrovac through the beautiful rocky scenery that lines the Montenegrin Coast. After about 15km it passes beneath the ruins of the former Turkish fortresses of Haj and Nehaj (200m (656ft)), and after another 2km arrives at **Sutomore**. The village provides an extensive shallow beach. The small river just to the south of it is the Zeljeznica, which until 1918 formed the border between Montenegro and the Austro-Hungarian Empire.

The road soon comes to the turning for **Bar** (Antivari). Bar is the biggest port in Montenegro, and is continuing to grow and thrive. It is at the terminus of the railway linking Titograd* (and ultimately Belgrade) with the coast. There is also a ferry to the Italian port of Bari. In spite of all the industry, the town has an extensive bathing beach.

Soon after the Bar turning, there is a left turn along a side-road that goes over the Sutorman Pass to Virpazar on Lake Scutari (see above), continuing as far as Rijeka-Crnojevica on the main road between Cetinje* and Titograd*.

Shortly after that there is another left turn for the old village of **Stari Bar**, which is situated among the olive groves on the slopes of the Rumija Mountains. The old site was originally Roman, but subsequently came under Byzantine and Venetian rule. It belonged to the Turks from the early sixteenth century until 1878, when it was mostly destroyed by gunfire from Montenegrin freedom-fighters. The medieval houses and fortifications were totally abandoned, but are now on view to the public. The new village of Stari Bar is built outside the old walls. It is worth a visit, especially on market days (usually

Market day at Stari Bar

Fridays), for the sake of its almost oriental way of life.

The coast road continues through a fertile region full of ancient olive trees and more recently planted orange and lemon groves. It is another 28km to **Ulcinj** (Dulcigno), the most southerly tourist resort on the Montenegrin Coast. The town clings to the slopes above the beach, and is typically surrounded by olive groves and pinewoods. Its Turkish houses and mosques add a distinctly oriental flavour.

Ulcinj was built on the site of a Roman settlement, and was destroyed by an earthquake in 1444. In the sixteenth century the Turks founded a pirate settlement here for a band of Algerian pirates. The town became notorious as a result. The black slaves that were brought here were the ancestors of Yugoslavia's native black population, who are still based in Ulcinj. The false messiah Sabbataj Zvi was exiled to Ulcinj for starting a religious movement among the Sephardic Jews; he died here in 1676.

The Turkish fortress was destroyed in 1878. Its ruins are still visible on a rock to the north of the bathing beach. They are surrounded by remnants of the old town, most of which was similarly destroyed. Apart from the bathing beach below the town, there is a sandy beach extending 12km to the south. It is lined by rows of hotels,

*Ulcinj, the most southerly resort
on the Montenegrin Coast*

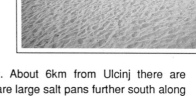

and includes a nudist colony. About 6km from Ulcinj there are sulphurous springs, and there are large salt pans further south along the coast.

The marshy region to the south of Ulcinj has been partially drained and cultivated. The Albanian border is formed by an outflow of Lake Scutari called the Bojana (in Albanian Buenë). The island in the delta is called Ada, and is the site for a nudist colony. The Yugoslav border village of **Sveti Nikola** lies a short distance upstream.

5 CITIES, TOWNS AND ISLANDS

Adelsberg Caves *see* **Postojna Caves**

Arbe *see* **Rab Island**

Biograd

Dalmatian Coast: Northern Section

B iograd is a small town of only a few thousand people. It was founded in the tenth century, and was the capital of the old kingdom of Croatia. It was destroyed by the Venetians in 1215. In 1646 it was again destroyed, this time by its own inhabitants as they fled the advancing Turks. Remains from these earlier settlements are on display in the municipal museum.

Biograd

There is a ferry service from Biograd to Tkon on the adjacent island of Pasman (see the Dalmatian Islands*). Apart from the old town, there is a colony of modern hotels next to an excellent beach. There is also a spacious marina.

An inland excursion to **Benkovac** (21km) is highly recommended, especially on market days (the tenth of every month). Benkovac is the main market centre of the karst plateau region of Ravni Kotari, where some excellent wines are produced. On a hill to the south-east is the ruined fortress of **Perusic**, which was important during the period of Turkish occupation.

Five kilometres east of Benkovac is the site of the former Roman city of Asseria. Twenty-one kilometres further to the south-east, on a hill near the village of **Bribir**, there is another Roman site called Varvaria. Items discovered at both these sites are on display at museums in Zadar* and Split*. Visitors to Varvaria are recommended to return to Biograd via Skradin, the Krka Falls and Sibenik*.

Brac Island (Formerly Brazza)

Dalmatian Coast: Central Section

Brac is the third-largest of the Yugoslavian islands (after Krk and Cres). Although only 40km long, it is up to 14km wide and has an area of 396sq km. The western tip is only 1km away from the island of Solta (see the Dalmatian Islands*). The highest point is the Vidova Gora (778m (2,552ft)).

The island is unusually fertile, and is consequently one of the most densely populated of the Yugoslavian islands. The inhabitants are distributed among fifty scattered villages and hamlets. The main products are wine and fruit, including figs and almonds; there are also olive trees, lavender and a plant called the buvac from which insecticides are made.

The quarries near Supetar once provided stone for the Palace of Diocletian at Split*. It is a kind of white limestone known as Brac marble because of its resemblance to marble; although initially soft, it becomes much harder when exposed to the air. Brac marble is still a major export to this day.

The island was first settled in prehistoric times. The Greeks and

Romans called it Brattia or Brachia. Many people fled here following the destruction of the Roman provincial capital of Salona. The island became Venetian in 1420, and since then its history has been much the same as that of the rest of the Dalmatian Coast.

Supetar is the main commercial centre of the island; it is linked by ferry to Split* on the mainland, and by bus to the other villages on the island. It is the most popular resort on Brac apart from Bol on the south coast. The many sandy beaches provide ideal bathing for children. The surroundings are very pleasant, with vineyards, pine-woods and tamarisk bushes. The cemetery contains a mausoleum built by the sculptor Rosandic for the famous Petrinovic family.

The tiny village of **Spliska** is 3km to the east, and within easy walking distance of Supetar. It is in a lovely woodland setting next to a bay, and has a small medieval church. The nearby quarries provided the building stone (Brac marble) for the Palace of Diocletian at Split*. The small hamlet of **Skrip** on the hillside above includes remains of some old houses and fortifications.

A short way further east is the beach resort of **Postira** which lies half-way along the north coast opposite the small mainland town of Omis. Surrounded by pinewoods and olive groves, it provides ideal bathing, especially from the nearby beach at Prvija.

Sutivan is 6km due west of Supetar and almost directly opposite Split. It is surrounded by parks and pinewoods, and there are two good beaches and many coves suitable for bathing along the coast.

Nerezisce is 9km south of Supetar in the centre of the island. Once the main town on the island, it is now only a tiny village. There are a few old villas, a n old town hall with a loggia, and a small church.

Milna lies 14km due west of Nerezisce, and is surrounded by pinewoods and olive groves at the head of a long inlet. Bathing is good, and there are plenty of lovely walks. There is a good view from the fourteenth-century chapel of Sveti Martin on the nearby hillside.

There is another road running eastwards from Nerezisce through the centre of the island. A side-road to the left leads to the village of **Pucisca** which lies at the head of an inlet on the north side of the island. It is a good place for fishing, and is surrounded by a number of limestone (Brac marble) quarries.

Another side-road runs south towards the lovely coastal resort of **Bol** which is served by a passenger boat from Split*. It is situated in a wine-producing area. The Dominican friary contains an interesting coin collection, and there is a painting by Tintoretto in the church. There are two lovely bathing beaches close by, plus a third one at the neighbouring promontory of Zlatni Rat. Its name means 'golden cape', which exactly describes this gently sloping sandy beach. Bol is also the starting point for the 2-hour climb to the top of the Vidova Gora (778m (2,552ft)), the highest point on the island. There is a magnificent view from the summit.

At the eastern end of the island is the small village of **Sumartin**. Its beaches are surrounded by forests, and look out across the channel to the mighty Biokovo Mountains on the mainland. The nearby village of **Selca** is another place where the so-called Brac marble is quarried.

North of Selca, the village of **Povlja** is situated next to an irregular-shaped bay. There are several good bathing beaches and plenty of good fishing for anglers.

Capodistria *see* **Koper**

Cattaro *see* **Kotor**

Cetinje

Montenegrin Coast

This former Montenegrin capital is at 672m (2,204ft) above sea level. Cetinje was founded in the mid-fifteenth century, and until 1916 was the seat of government for the small principality of Montenegro.

Next to the Trg Marsaia Tita (Marshal Tito Square) is the old **Biljarda Palace**, built 1832, formerly the residence of Peter II. It now contains the Njegos Museum, the Museum of Ethnography and the Museum of the Liberation Struggle. An adjoining building contains a large relief of Montenegro. The former palace of King Nikola houses the **Municipal Museum**, with collections of weapons, war trophies, costumes and paintings.

The convent church of **Sveti Petar** was originally built in the fifteenth century. Though destroyed by the Turks, it was subsequently rebuilt, and contains the first-ever book to have been printed in the Cyrillic alphabet, in 1493. The church of **Vlaska Crkva** was also built in the fifteenth century. The metal fence surrounding it was forged from Turkish weapons.

The small town also includes a number of former embassy buildings which, though modest in size, are an indication of its former importance.

It is 47km from Cetinje to the modern provincial capital of Titograd*. The road first crosses the Belvedere Pass, from which there is a particularly good view, then drops down into **Rijeka-Crnojevica**. Overlooking the village are the ruins of Obod Monastery, which was the home of the first Southern Slav printing press.

There is also an old stone bridge from the period of Turkish occupation. There is a right turn here along a small mountain road to Virpazar on Lake Scutari (33km); it continues over the Sutorman Pass (844m (2,768ft)), with some magnificent views, and eventually comes out at the coastal town of Bar (another 22km; see the Montenegrin Coast).

Cetinje is only 38km from Kotor*. The route runs through magnificent scenery along the north-western side of the Lovcen massif (see page 139). There is a third road across the mountains to the coastal resort of Budva (see the Montenegrin Coast).

Cres and Losinj (Formerly Cherso and Lussigno)

Istria

With an area of 400sq km, **Cres** is the second-largest of Yugoslavia's thousand or so islands. It is one of the group known as the Kvarner Islands. The eastern coast is steep and barren, while the west coast is gentler by comparison. Most of the villages are situated on the western side, including Cres, Martinscica and Osor.

The island is 68km long and measures 12km at the widest point. This is roughly in the middle of the island, where there is a large freshwater lake called the Vransko Jezero. The north of Cres supports only sparse woodlands and bushes, while the southern part is noticeably more fertile. The main crops are wine and olives, and also some vegetables. The highest point (650m (2,132ft)) is towards the northern end of the island.

Cres was inhabited in prehistoric times. The Illyrians were followed by the Greeks and Romans, who called the island Crexa. It belonged to the Venetians almost permanently from about AD 1000 down to 1797, and then to Austria until 1918. The island was part of Italy during the interwar period, but was eventually handed over to Yugoslavia.

The main road on the island runs from Porozina in the north as far as Osor, where it crosses to the neighbouring island of Losinj (see below). The small hamlet of **Porozina** faces the eastern coast of Istria, and is the ferry terminus for boats from the mainland ports of Brestova and Rijeka*.

Twenty-six kilometres further south is the small fishing port of **Cres** (Cherso), which is the main town on the island. Parts of the old fortification walls have been preserved, including an old defence tower. Next to the harbour are the old town hall, a Renaissance loggia and a sixteenth-century bell tower. The parish church of Sveta Marija and the nearby Franciscan monastery both contain some beautiful paintings. The municipal museum has some interesting Graeco-Roman amphoras. There are some lovely old Venetian houses in the old part of the town. One of the many neighbouring beaches has been set aside for nudists.

Further south along the coast is the fishing village of **Valun**, which is situated by a bay of the same name. Valun is the site where a famous eleventh-century Glagolitic inscription was discovered.

The village of **Vrana** lies in the centre of the island about 18km south of Cres, at the point where the main road touches the southern tip of the **Vransko Jezero**. This freshwater lake is strange in having no visible feeder rivers apart from a few tiny streams; it is thought to be supplied by underground streams that flow under the sea from the mainland. It is 5km long by 2km wide, and has a maximum depth of 84m (275ft). It is full of fish, and provides drinking water for both the islands of Cres and Losinj.

The farming and fishing village of **Martinscica** lies on the nearby west coast next to a south-facing bay. The old castle has been converted into a restaurant, and there are several rocky beaches.

Osor is the second-largest village on the island (after Cres). It is situated 20km south of Vrana next to the channel running between Cres and Losinj. It is only 9m (29$\frac{1}{2}$ft wide at this point, and the main road crosses to Losinj via a short swingbridge. The village has a long and illustrious history, as is shown by the Roman remains on display in the museum (formerly the town hall). The old houses and the medieval church also indicate that Osor was once very much larger. Indeed, the port of Osero, as it was then called, had a population of some 20,000. The old Venetian walls are still partly preserved. The fifteenth-century parish church contains a fascinating Venetian altarpiece, while the church of Sveti Gaudencije includes the remains of some old frescos.

A small road crosses the island from Osor to the tiny east-coast village of **Punta Kriza** (10km), which is perched high above an irregular-shaped inlet. This is a part of the island that has not yet been opened up to tourists.

The island of **Losinj** has an area of 80sq km, and is thus only a fifth the size of Cres. But with double the population of its larger neighbour, it is far more important from the tourist's point of view. Losinj became a popular holiday retreat as early as 1900 on account of its favourable climate and the beautiful villages along the coast. It is 31km long and up to 5km wide. The inhabitants are divided between ten villages, the largest of which are the bathing resorts of Mali Losinj and Veli Losinj.

Losinj, like Cres, was familiar to the Greeks, whose name for it was Apsyrtides. But it is not known whether the island was inhabited at that time. All that is certain is that Slavs settled here in the thirteenth century. Since that time its history has been much the same as that of its larger neighbour.

The first resort along the road from Cres is **Nerezine**. This ancient coastal settlement is bounded to the east by a Franciscan monastery. To the west is the highest point of the island, the Televrina (588m (1,928ft)), with a marvellous view from the summit.

Twenty kilometres further south is the main town on the island, **Mali Losinj** (Lussin Piccolo). Though the first element of the name means 'little', it is nowadays larger than Veli (= 'great') Losinj. The resort of Mali Losinj has been famous for more than a century. It is situated at the head of a 5km-long inlet, and is overlooked by the ruined sixteenth-century fortifications. A church with a bell tower is perched on a hill above them. The surrounding woodlands and meadows are ideal for walks. The nearest beach is at Cikat, which is 2km away on the west coast of the island. Of the five other neighbouring bathing beaches, one has been turned into a nudist colony.

Veli Losinj is 4km south-east of Mali Losinj, and is pleasantly situated at the foot of a hill (243m (797ft)). The parish church was founded in the fifteenth century and restored in the eighteenth; there are some beautiful paintings inside. The fourteenth-century church of Sveti Nikola contains some equally valuable paintings. The old Uskok tower in the centre of the village was restored in the seventeenth century. Several villas were built here at the turn of the century when tourism began to expand. They include the former summer residence of Archduke Karl Stefan of Austria, which is surrounded by beautiful subtropical gardens (not always open to the public). There are some lovely walks through the surrounding woodlands, and a number of good beaches for bathing.

There are several smaller islands to the west and south of Losinj; they can be reached by boat from Osor or Mali Losinj. **Unije** (Unie) to the north-west has an area of 18sq km. The only village on the island is Unije, on the west coast next to a good bathing beach.

The island of **Susak** (Sansego) to the west is even smaller, with an area of only 4sq km. It is remarkable in being made of sand instead

Mali Losinj on the Island of Losinj

Veli Losinj

of rock. The sand is built up in terraces, and has gradually been hardened into loess. The trees are naturally very few, but the wines are very good. There are also a lot of reeds growing around the island. The village of Susak is overlooked by the remains of a tower that once belonged to a fortified Benedictine abbey. Susak clings hard to its old customs, and the local women's costumes are especially beautiful.

The small but hilly island of **Ilovik** lies just off the southern tip of Losinj. It is separated by a narrow channel from the even smaller island of **Sveti Petar** (San Pietro), which lies opposite the small fishing village of Ilovik. The remains of an eleventh-century Benedictine abbey are still visible on Sveti Petar.

Dalmatian Islands

Dalmatian Coast

These islands extend along the Dalmatian Coast of Yugoslavia from Pag opposite Karlobag in the north to Kolocep near Dubrovnik in the south. The largest of the islands are dealt with separately. They are Pag*, Brac*, Hvar* and Korcula*, not forgetting the nearby Peljesac Peninsula*. The rest of them are relatively small, and have therefore been dealt with together here.

Many of the islands described below are uninhabited, while others have a single village with the same name as the island. But even the smallest of them can provide a pleasant, relaxing holiday in the sun, away from all the bustle of the busier resorts. Visitors must, however, be happy with their own company, and must be prepared for fairly primitive conditions. This often means making do without running water or electricity and many of the other luxuries they are used to at home

The islands enjoy a favourable climate. They are wooded, especially in the south, and the vegetation is predominantly subtropical. The people live mainly from fishing and sailing, wine and olive production, plus a certain amount of livestock.

Some of the islands are served by ferries from the mainland, and boat excursions are organised to many of the others. One of the most interesting places is the Kornat Archipelago — a vast patchwork of small islets, rocks and reefs, providing a paradise for anglers and divers.

The islands are considered here in geographical order, going from north to south. They are divided into two main groups separated by a gap. The North Dalmatian Islands are often small, but are correspondingly numerous; they extend as far as Sibenik*. The South Dalmatian Islands are much fewer but somewhat larger; they begin roughly on a level with Marina (west of Trogir*).

Olib, Silba and Premuda

These three islands are the most northerly of the Dalmatian Islands apart from Pag*. They continue the chain of islands that begins in the north with Cres* and Losinj.

The island of **Olib** is larger than many, with an area of 29sq km. The main village, also called Olib is situated next to a bay on the west coast, and offers good bathing. There is another somewhat larger bathing beach on the east coast of the island.

Silba lies immediately to the west of Olib, and has an area of 15sq km. The name is derived from the Latin word *silva* meaning 'woodland'. It is no longer covered in woodland, but the vegetation is lush, consisting of shrubs and bushes, orchards and olive groves. The fishing village of Silba is situated at the narrowest point of the island. There are some fine paintings in the village church. There are pleasant bathing beaches either side of the isthmus on which the village is built.

Premuda is the smallest of the three islands, with an area of only 9sq km. It lies west of Silba, and so is the furthest from the coast. It is the most northerly of the outermost chain of islands running south-east via Dugi Otok and the Kornat Archipelago to Zirje off Sibenik. The village is also called Premuda.

Molat and Sestrunj

South of Premuda, the islands of **Skarda**, **Ist** and **Molat** (in that order) are not particularly important for tourists. Molat is the largest, having an area of 22sq km. It is irregular in shape, and reaches a maximum height of 142m (466ft).

The next island to the south is **Sestrunj**, with an area of 14sq km. Next to it are the tiny islands of **Rivanj** to the east, **Zverinac** and **Tun** to the west.

Dugi Otok

The name means 'long island' and is an apt description for Dugi Otok, which is 44km long, up to 5km wide and has a total area of 125sq km. The highest point is the Vela Straza (338m (1,108ft)), roughly at the mid-point of the island. Dugi Otok is situated 15km from the mainland; the northern end is approximately level with Nin (north of Zadar), and the southern end with Filip-Jakov (south of Zadar). Zadar* itself is hidden by the intervening islands of Ugljan and Iz (see below).

Most of the ten villages on Dugi Otok are on the east side of the island facing the mainland. The west side is mainly barren, while the coast at either end is extremely irregular. The main villages are Soline, Bozava, Luka and Sali, all of which provide a certain amount of simple accommodation.

Soline lies at the head of a long inlet at the northern end of the island. The bathing is good here, though it is even better in the nearby Saharun Inlet. **Bozava** is at the northern end of the east coast, surrounded by pine forests. It provides the best of the island's modest tourist facilities. The parish church contains some interesting proces-

The cliffs of Dugi Otok

sional crosses. Also of interest is the small tenth-century chapel of
Sveti Nikola.

The fishing village of **Luka** and the chief village of **Sali** are towards the southern end of the island. Sali has good bathing facilities, and is a good place from which to visit the Kornat Islands (see below).

Ugljan

The island of Ugljan lies across the channel from Zadar*. It is 22km long by up to 4km wide, and has an area of 46sq km. The highest point is the Veliko Brdo (288m (944ft)), and the west coast is very steep. Most of the villages are situated on the eastern side of the island; they are all linked by roads.

The fishing village of **Ugljan** is situated towards the northern end of the east coast. It has a Franciscan monastery with an interesting fifteenth-century cloister. Further south along the coast is another fishing village called **Lukoran** which offers a number of pleasant bathing beaches surrounded by pinewoods. The small cemetery chapel dates back to the eleventh century.

Preko is the island's main port and commercial centre. It is situated directly opposite Zadar*, and there is a ferry service linking the two. There is a fine beach, making it a popular destination for day-visitors from Zadar. There is a good view from the nearby Venetian fortress of Sveti Mihovil. There are two small islands off Preko: **Galovac**, with a little old Franciscan friary surrounded by woods, and **Osljak**, with the remains of an old windmill.

The fishing village of **Kali** is only 3km further down the coast, and is also popular with tourists. The most southerly fishing village is **Kukljica** which provides a good beach and holiday accommodation. It is not far from the narrow Zdrelac Strait that divides Ugljan from the neighbouring island of Pasman, and which is spanned by a bridge linking the two islands.

Pasman

Pasman is the same length as Ugljan, but is generally wider, giving a greater total area. The island is hilly, reaching a maximum height of 274m (900ft).

The villages are again situated on the east side of the island facing the mainland. They are linked by a road running along the coast from the Zdrelac Strait to the ferry port of Tkon. They all provide good bathing, and are popular with day-trippers from Biograd*. Apart from the tiny hamlets of Zdrelac, Nevidjane and Kraj, there are the

Yachting on the Dalmatian Coast

larger fishing villages of Pasman and Tkon, both of which provide boat trips and fishing expeditions to the Kornat Islands (see below).

The main village of **Pasman** is roughly half-way down the coast. The people live mostly from fishing, but also to a certain extent from agriculture. There are several prehistoric sites in the area around, and the bathing facilities are good. **Tkon** lies towards the southern end of the island; it is directly opposite Biograd*, to which it is linked by ferry. Some Roman tombs have been found nearby, and there is a Benedictine abbey to the north-west.

Iz and Zut

The small island of Iz lies mid-way between Dugi Otok and Ugljan; it is 12km long and 2km wide. The main village of **Iz Veli** is famous for its pottery. It has a good beach with hotel and guesthouse accommodation, and is a popular retreat for anglers. The smaller village of **Iz Mali** has an old Croatian church.

South-east of Iz are the small islands of **Lavarda**, **Sit** and **Zut**. Zut is the largest of the three, and is associated with a whole group of much smaller islands.

The Kornat Archipelago

The main island of the group is **Kornat**, which is 24km long and up to 2km wide. It lies west of Zut, and forms the southern continuation of the Dugi Otok chain. The island includes the remains of a medieval castle and an early Christian basilica.

The Kornat Archipelago stretches 40km to the south-east. It consists of more than 150 tiny islands, some of them no more than rocks. Many are totally uninhabited, while others are only inhabited in the summer. A very few have enough soil for growing olives or wine, or to provide a small amount of grazing for sheep.

The chief attraction lies in the water around the islands, which, being extremely clear, is ideal for fishing and diving. The rocks and cliffs are particularly beautiful, and are full of hidden coves and grottos. Boat trips are organised from nearby ports such as Zadar* and Sibenik* — some of them for anglers and others for sightseeing.

Murter

This is the name of a small island lying immediately off the coast between Biograd* and Sibenik*. It is 11km long and 2km wide and is linked to the mainland via a bridge. The scenery is beautiful, making it well worth a short excursion.

The bridge crosses to the island near the village of **Tijesno**, where there are several beaches among the pinewoods. Not far away is the tiny village of **Jezero**, which also has a pleasant sheltered beach. At the northern end of the island are the fishing village of **Betina** and the main village of **Murter**. The bathing resort of **Slanica** is ideally situated next to a shallow sandy bay.

The Islands off Sibenik

The most southerly of the North Dalmatian Islands are a group lying off the coast around Sibenik*. The first of these is the small island of

Prvic, which lies immediately off the coast opposite the small town of Vodice. There are two tiny villages on this island.

The main island in front of Sibenik itself is **Zlarin**, where traditional costumes are still worn. There is a good beach surrounded by greenery near the village of Zlarin. Apart from agriculture, wine and sea fishing, the inhabitants still follow the centuries-old customs of mud and coral fishing. Mud fishing is similarly practised by the menfolk on the island of **Krapanj** between Zlarin and the coast.

There are many more islands further out to sea, most of them uninhabited; the main ones are **Tijat**, **Zamajan**, **Kaprije** and **Kakanj**. The largest of the group is **Zirje**, which is also the furthest west; it has an area of 17sq km.

The Drvenik Islands
The first of the South Dalmatian Islands are the tiny island of **Drvenik Mali** (area 4sq km) and its somewhat larger neighbour **Drvenik Veli** (12sq km). They are situated off the central Dalmatian Coast on a level with the village of Marina west of Trogir. The inhabitants live mostly from agriculture.

Betina, Murter Island

Ciovo

The island of Ciovo lies immediately off Trogir* itself, to which it is linked via a bridge. It has an area of 30sq km, and extends east towards Split* in front of the Kastelanski Riviera. There are six villages on the island. The largest of these is **Ciovo** itself, which is effectively a suburb of Trogir. Four kilometres east of the bridge is the monastery of Sveti Kriz (St Cross). The next most important community is **Slatine**, from which there is a marvellous view across the Bay of Seven Castles. Just to the south of Ciovo Island is the tiny uninhabited island of **Kraljevac**.

Solta

The island of Solta lies due south of Ciovo and 15km south-west of Split*; it is popular with day-visitors from the coast. The island is hilly, reaching a maximum height of 208m (682ft), and there are ten small villages to be found there. Some of the soils are very fertile, and it was inhabited during Greek and Roman times. The remains of Roman villas have been found scattered all over the island, including some fine mosaic floors.

The fishing village of **Maslinica** is situated on the west coast of the island. It includes the ruins of an old watch tower built to guard against pirates, and an eighteenth-century noble residence. The tiny island of **Stipanska** off the coast is the site of a ruined medieval convent.

A road crosses the island to the main village of **Grohote**, which is situated in the middle of the island. There are a number of Roman remains in the vicinity. Only 2km to the north is the main island port of **Rogac**, which is situated next to a pretty inlet on the north coast. It is served by ferries from Split*.

The main road continues east from Grohote to the fishing village of **Necujam** which lies on the north coast next to an irregular-shaped inlet of the same name. The bathing facilities are excellent. The adjoining park is covered with fine woodlands and subtropical vegetation. It forms the estate of the former residence of the sixteenth-century poet Marko Marulic, which is still in good condition.

Further east along the coast is the small village of **Stomorska** where the remains of Roman sarcophagi can be seen in the cemetery. The beach here is similarly good for bathing.

Vis (formerly Lissa)

Vis lies about 20km south-west of Hvar*. It is the largest of the most outlying group of islands, and has an area of 60sq km. The island is steep and hilly, and the highest point is a hill called the Hum (585m (1919ft)). The coast is correspondingly steep and rocky, but forms two sheltered bays for the ports of Vis and Komiza. The climate is very pleasant, favouring wine and fruit cultivation. The rich subtropical vegetation includes palms, eucalyptus, agaves, cacti, oranges, lemons and mimosas. However, some of the island is still covered by restricted military zones.

Vis was the first island along the coast to be settled by the Greeks, who called it Issa. It was later taken over by the Romans, and its subsequent history is bound up with that of Dalmatia. Known to the Venetians as Lissa, it was dubbed the Malta of the Adriatic on account of its strategic importance. In 1811 it was conquered by the British from the French following a decisive sea battle. In 1866 Admiral Tegethoff of Austria routed a superior Italian fleet in the waters off the island. In World War II it became a vital Yugoslav stronghold, and Marshal Tito had his headquarters here for a while.

The small town of **Vis** is situated next to an inlet on the north coast of the island. It is guarded by old fortifications, mostly from the period of British occupation. Not far away are some archaeological remains of the ancient Greek colony of Issa.

A road crosses the island to **Komiza**, which lies on the west coast immediately below the Hum. It is somewhat larger than Vis, and has a significant fish-canning industry. There is an old sixteenth-century fort by the shore. Also of interest are the churches of Gospa Gusarica and Sveti Nikola, which contains some impressive paintings. The extensive pebble beach offers good bathing facilities.

Bisevo and Svetac

The tiny island of **Bisevo** lies south-west of Vis, and has an area of barely 6sq km. It is popular with tourists on account of the famous Modra Spilja or Blue Grotto. This cave is 31m (102ft) long; the narrow entrance is half-submerged, and is only passable when the sea is completely calm. Glorious colours are produced by the reflection and refraction of sunlight at the entrance; they are best in the late morning.

There are several more rocky islets further out to sea. Of these, **Jabuka** is little more than a rock protuding 96m (315ft) from the sea; **Svetac** is somewhat bigger, climbing to 305m (1,000ft), and is the site of a small fishing village. These and other outlying islands are good centres for tunny and lobster fishing. Bisevo, Jabuka and Svetac, are occupied by military zones.

Lastovo (formerly Lagosta)

The wooded island of Lastovo lies 13km south of Korcula*. It is 11km long and up to 6km wide, with a total area of 47sq km. The island is popular on account of the good fishing to be found there. It is also famous for its fine wines, known as Plavac. Traditional dress is still worn on festival days. Until recently Lastovo was a military zone and forbidden to foreigners.

The main village of **Lastovo** clings to the hillside above the north coast of the island. The parish church and the loggia date back to the fourteenth and fifteenth centuries. The local harbour is formed by the nearby Bay of Sveti Mihovil.

The main port, however, is **Ubli** to the south-west, which is built on a very old site. The bathing here is similarly good. The south coast of the island is rocky and uninhabited. The lighthouse on the Struga Point was built in 1849.

There are numerous rocks and islets both to the east and west of Lastovo. They are used for lobster fishing, and the largest of them are **Kopiste** and **Susac**.

Mljet (formerly Melita)

This somewhat larger island lies to the east of Lastovo and south of the Peljesac Peninsula*. It is 38km long and up to 4km wide, with a total area of 100sq km. Interestingly, the island is of volcanic origin, and the highest point is the Veliki Grad (514m (1,686ft)). The surface is largely wooded and the coast is irregular. One remarkable feature of the island fauna is the mongoose, which was introduced from India to keep down the snake population.

The Romans called the island Melita, and used it as a place of banishment. In the Middle Ages it belonged to several different Serbian rulers. In the fourteenth century it became part of Ragusa (Dubrovnik), and in 1572 it was laid waste by the Turks.

At the well, Mljet

The western part of the island has been turned into a nature reserve or national park. It includes two remarkable lakes called the **Veliko Jezero** and **Malo Jezero** ('great lake' and 'small lake'). A narrow channel links the two lakes together, while a second even narrower channel links the Veliko Jezero to the sea on the south side of the island. The latter channel is so narrow that the slight movement of the tides creates a current along it. Monks from the nearby Benedictine abbey (on an island in the lake) built a mill over this channel to make use of the water power. The mill has long since fallen into ruin, but the abbey has been turned into an exclusive hotel.

The small village of **Govedjari** is close by on the north side of the Veliko Jezero. The tiny port of **Polace** lies a short way further north by an inlet adjoining the north coast; next to it are the remains of a large Roman palace. The biggest village on the island is **Babino Polje**, which is situated below the Veliki Grad on the eastern edge of the national park. A road runs along the centre of the island, linking the villages together.

The beautiful Dalmatian island of Mljet

The Deer Islands

The small islands to the north-west of Dubrovnik* form the last group of the South Dalmatian Islands. All of them are popular with day-trippers from Dubrovnik and its associated resorts.

Sipan lies immediately off the coast opposite the villages of Slano and Trsteno. It is the largest island of the group, having an area of 20sq km. Of the two villages on the island, **Sudjuradj** is situated at the south-eastern end. It includes two former palaces, an eleventh-century church and the remains of a Benedictine abbey. **Luka**, the most popular village, lies next to an inlet on the south side of the island. It similarly possesses some old palaces and chapels.

Opposite Luka and guarding the entrance to the inlet is the small island of **Jakljan**, which is similarly wooded. Several Roman sites

Dubrovnik's harbour

have been discovered here, together with later buildings from the period of rule from Dubrovnik (Ragusa).

The small island of **Lopud** to the south-east of Sipan has an area of only 5sq km. But the one village of Lopud is a popular holiday retreat, especially with foreign visitors. This is mostly on account of its lush green vegetation and shallow sandy beach. The village provides a certain amount of hotel accommodation, and there is a pleasant area of old parkland alongside the harbour. There are additional bathing facilities on the opposite side of the island next to the Bay of Sunj. The island itself is dotted with the remains of old chapels and palaces, many of them medieval in origin.

The tiny island **Kolocep** is only 7km from Dubrovnik*. The two small fishing villages of Gornje Celo and Donje Celo are surrounded by subtropical vegetation. There are several excellent bathing beaches in beautiful surroundings. Kolocep also has a number of ruined medieval houses and chapels.

Lopud

Dubrovnik (Formerly Ragusa)

Dalmatian Coast: Southern Section

The city of Dubrovnik lies in really beautiful surroundings. The warm climate encourages a rich growth of subtropical vegetation, including agaves, palms, pines, cypresses, olives, figs, oranges, lemons, oleanders and camellias. Thanks to its unusually mild winters, Dubrovnik is an ideal resort for winter and early spring holidays.

The former city of Ragusa bears witness to an eventful history spanning 1,300 years, while the modern town of Dubrovnik offers a wide variety of modern hotels, festivals and other events, together with all the bustle and life of a port and seaside resort. In few other towns are the past and the present so effectively matched as in this thriving port with its beautiful old walled city.

The city was founded in the seventh century AD by refugees fleeing from the nearby Graeco-Roman city of Epidaurus (now

Cavtat) following its destruction by the Avars. It took the name of the small island of Ragusa on which it was built, and from the very beginning the people lived primarily from the sea. Slav immigrants also came to settle among the oakwoods (*dubrova*) on the adjacent mainland. In the twelfth century the island was linked with the mainland, uniting the Latin city of Ragusa with the adjoining Slav settlement of Dubrova.

The city maintained its independence by acknowledging the sovereignty of one state after another — first the Byzantine Empire, then Venice and Hungary and finally even the Ottoman Turks. This clever policy entailed no more than the payment of a tribute — a sum which was more than recompensed by the city's enormous prosperity. Ragusa remained independent until 1808, when Napoléon dissolved the senate and absorbed it into the Illyrian Provinces. In 1814 Austria took over, but in 1918 Dubrovnik finally became part of the new Yugoslav state.

The fifteenth century was Ragusa's golden age. The political power lay with the nobility, who formed the senate. The main chamber of the senate elected a new rector or leader every month. They also elected an inner chamber or cabinet, who ruled in conjunction with the rector. An old people's home was built here as early as the fourteenth century, and slavery was abolished in the fifteenth century. The great earthquake of 1667 killed 5,000 people and destroyed many of the old buildings, including the cathedral. But the old city has nonetheless preserved much of its medieval profile.

The old city of Dubrovnik is built on a promontory that was originally an island (see above), and is enclosed by massive medieval fortifications. The eastern suburb is called Ploce, while the more modern suburbs of Pile, Gruz and Lapad stretch out to the northwest. The inlet at Gruz forms Dubrovnik's main harbour.

The suburbs spread out along the slopes of the 412m-high (1,351ft) Brdo Srdj, which is crowned by a massive French fortress built in 1809. There is a magnificent view from the top overlooking the city, the coast and the sea. It can be reached by cable car or by 1¹/₂ hours' climb on foot. A further half-hour on foot brings one via Bosanka to the Zarkovica viewing point (312m (1,023ft)).

A circuit of the old city walls is highly recommended for the wonderful views they provide. The best place to start is the Ploce

Fortress and old harbour, Dubrovnik

Church spire and red roof-tops, Dubrovnik

Gate in the east. This is the only land entrance to the old town apart from the Pile Gate to the west and a more recently built road entrance below the Kula Sveti Jakov (St Jacob's Tower). (One can of course enter by boat from the sea via the old harbour.) There are two fortresses standing outside the old walls: the Tvrdjava Lovrijene on a rock out to the west, and the Tvrdjava Revelin just to the east of the Ploce Gate.

Visitors are recommended to enter the old city on foot from the Brsalije Square to the west, where there is parking available. A series of steps leads across the old moat and enters the city through the sixteenth-century Pile Gate. A broad street called the Placa or Stadrun runs straight through the old city from here to the harbour. This was once the channel dividing Ragusa from the mainland, which was completely filled in after the great earthquake of 1677.

The first building on the right is the beautiful **Onofrio Fountain** — a domed structure with sixteen waterspouts, dating back to 1438. Behind it is the old thirteenth-century convent of **Sveta Klara**, where Europe's first orphanage was founded in 1432. Opposite is the small Renaissance chapel of **Sveti Spas** (St Saviour), built in 1520. Its beautiful façade was created by the Andrijic brothers.

The building next to it is a fourteenth-century Franciscan monastery, whose magnificent late Gothic west door was carved by the Petrovic brothers. The lower cloister is especially worth seeing, and was built by Miho of Bar. It also contains one of the oldest pharmacies in Europe, which was founded in 1318 and has been preserved in its original state. A staircase leads from here to the upper cloister. The church tower was built in 1424. The monastery also contains a library with a collection of old manuscripts and pictures, including a painting of the city before the great earthquake.

The eastern end of the Placa widens out into a square called the Poljana Luza, to the left of which is the impressive sixteenth-century **Palaca Sponza**. This building includes a columned arcade and a fine inner courtyard. It was originally the currency and customs headquarters, and later became a scholarly academy. It is nowadays used as an exhibition hall, while the city archives are kept in the rooms upstairs.

Straight ahead is the 31m-high (102ft) city tower, which guards the way through to the old harbour. Every hour the bell is struck by the two bronze figures either side. In front of it and to the right is **Roland's Column** (Orlandov Stup), built in the fifteenth century as the sign of the city's freedom. Close by is a smaller version of the

Onofrio Fountain, also dating from 1438.

Further to the right is the church of **Sveti Vlaho** (St Blasius), the patron saint of the city. Its original fourteenth-century structure was destroyed by fire, and it was rebuilt in the Baroque style at the beginning of the eighteenth century. One of its most interesting features is a statue of the saint himself holding a model of the city in his hand.

Behind the church is the nineteenth-century town hall, with a coffee bar in the basement called the Gradska Kavana. Next to it are the theatre and the **Rector's Palace** (Knezev Dvor). This impressive fifteenth-century structure was built in the late Gothic style by Onofrio de la Cava together with Michelozzo and Juraj Dalmatinac. Only 30 years later it was badly damaged by fire; the restoration work took account of the newly-emerging Renaissance style, as is clearly shown by the façade. This was the most important building in the town; the chambers of the senate assembled here, and it also served as the rector's residence. It now houses the municipal museum, which is also well worth a visit.

Somewhat to the right of the Rector's Palace is the Baroque cathedral (velika gospa), which contains paintings by Flemish masters and pupils of Titian, plus an unusually rich collection of other treasures. The **Bishop's Palace** (Biskupski Dvor) stands on the opposite side of the square, and houses a small collection of paintings.

Continuing to the left of the Bishop's Palace, one quickly comes out at the south-eastern point of the old city, where the **Tvrdjava Sveta Ivana** (St John's Fort) guards the entrance to the old harbour. It nowadays contains the Ethnographic and Maritime Museum and an aquarium.

If one returns to the Rector's Palace and continues westwards, one soon comes into another square called the Gunduliceva Poljana, where there is a statue of the Ragusan poet Ivan Gundulic (1588–1638). A narrow street called the Ulica od Puca leads westwards to a nineteenth-century Serbian Orthodox church, where the priest's house contains an interesting icon collection.

Going south out of the Gunduliceva Poljana, one comes to a steep flight of steps leading up to the Poljana Boskovica. To the right of this square is a Jesuit church (Jezuitska crkva), built in the

Narrow streets in the old city of Dubrovnik

eighteenth-century in the Baroque style.

If one returns to the Poljana Luza and continues north-east past the Palaca Sponza, one eventually arrives at a Dominican friary. Though founded in the fourteenth century, it was not finished until the sixteenth. The fifteenth-century church contains some valuable paintings, including Titian's *Maria Magdalena*. The late Gothic cloister was also built in the fifteenth century. The friary is close to the Ploce Gate, from which one can return to the Brsalje Square via the city walls (see above).

Pile, to the west of the old city, is the main commercial centre of Dubrovnik. Apart from several hotels, there is a large tourist information office giving information about all there is to do and see. Further out towards the harbour at Gruz (Gravosa) is the **Gradac** municipal park. **Boninovo** is a viewing point on a large rock overlooking the sea. To the south of the harbour, the **Lapad Peninsula** is nowadays covered with hotels, and there is a pleasant bathing beach at **Sumartin**.

Out to the east beyond **Ploce**, the slopes of Sveti Jakov provide the classic picture-postcard view of the old city, with the modern suburbs spreading out along the coast either side.

Also worth visiting is the island of **Lokrum** — a dome of rock covered in woodlands, and lying just off the coast to the south of Dubrovnik. It is popular with tourists, being only 15 minutes away by ferry. There is no accommodation on the island, which has been designated a nature reserve on account of its marvellous subtropical vegetation. Strict regulations are in force to preserve the flora intact. Smoking, for example, is strictly forbidden, as even a small fire could threaten the very existence of this Mediterranean paradise. One item of special interest is a small castle built by Archduke Maximilian next to a former Benedictine monastery. Other features include a darkgreen lake, a remarkable bridge formed by natural erosion, and a fascinating cave. On the highest point of the island (91m (298ft)) are the remains of the Fort Royale, part of the town's Napoleonic defences.

There is a ferry from Dubrovnik to the Italian Adriatic port of Bari. There are further sea connections to other towns along the coast such as Kotor, Split and Rijeka, and to many of the offshore islands.

One important place to visit from Dubrovnik is the small inland town of **Trebinje**. Although only 31km from the coast, and at a height of only 294m (964ft), its situation among the bare karst peaks makes

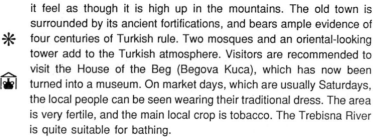

it feel as though it is high up in the mountains. The old town is surrounded by its ancient fortifications, and bears ample evidence of four centuries of Turkish rule. Two mosques and an oriental-looking tower add to the Turkish atmosphere. Visitors are recommended to visit the House of the Beg (Begova Kuca), which has now been turned into a museum. On market days, which are usually Saturdays, the local people can be seen wearing their traditional dress. The area is very fertile, and the main local crop is tobacco. The Trebisna River is quite suitable for bathing.

Fiume *see* **Rijeka**

Hvar Island (Formerly Lesina)

Dalmatian Coast: Central Section

Hvar is the same length as Cres* (68km), and is the longest of the Dalmatian Islands. Its width varies from 4km to 11km, and the total area is 300sq km. The highest point on the island is Sveti Nikola (626m (2,053ft)). The southern shore is very steep, while the north coast is much gentler but somewhat irregular. Hvar is often compared to Madeira on account of its mild climate — and not without reason; for the statistics show that its temperatures are the most favourable on the Dalmatian Coast apart from Dubrovnik.

The many Stone and Bronze Age finds show that the island was settled very early. In 385 BC the Greeks founded the colony of Pharos on the site of present-day Starigrad. The island was later settled by the Illyrians, who then fell to the Romans in 221 BC. The Slavs settled here in the eighth and ninth centuries AD, since when the island's history has been much the same as that of Dalmatia. Its period of greatest prosperity was between the fourteenth and sixteenth centuries during the period of Venetian rule. The Venetians called the island Lesina, but the Slav name is derived from the original Greek name Pharos.

The most important tourist resorts are Hvar, Starigrad, Vrboska and Jelsa. A road runs practically the whole length of the island, linking the towns and villages together. There are ferry connections from Split* to Vira and Starigrad, and from Drvenik to Sucuraj. There

Palace Hotel, Vira

are further boat links with the neighbouring islands of Brac*, Korcula* and Vis (see the Dalmatian Islands*).

The main agricultural products are wine, olive oil and fruit. Figs, carobs, oranges and lemons also flourish on the island. It is covered by large swathes of pine forest, but there are also areas of bush forest, where rosemary, lavender and other aromatic plants are cultivated.

The main centre on the island is the small town of **Hvar**. One of the best-known of all the Adriatic resorts, it is situated at the western end of the island, and is linked to Split* on the mainland via the nearby ferry port of **Vira**. It is patronised by tourists throughout the year, and the mild winter climate makes it an ideal winter resort.

The town nestles among the lush subtropical woodlands on a hill slope overlooking a small sheltered bay. It is guarded by two fortresses perched on the hillside above. The Spanish Fort (Tvrdjava Spanjola; 88m (288ft)) was built by Charles V in 1551; it is surrounded by fine parklands with some magnificent views. Fort St Nicolas (Tvrdjava Sveti Nikola; 230m (754ft)) is also known as Fort Napoléon, and was built by the French in 1806.

The loggia by the square next to the harbour was built by Sanmicheli in the sixteenth century; it now houses the kursaal together with a small café. Behind it are the massive Palace Hotel, and next to it a fifteenth-century bell tower. Across the square is a former sixteenth-century arsenal that was converted in 1612 into what is now the oldest theatre in Yugoslavia. There is also an old cistern in the square. Among the streets to the north are the ruins of a former Venetian mansion called the Hektorovic or Leporini Palace.

The cathedral stands at the eastern end of the square. Its bell tower is Romanesque, but the rest of the structure is sixteenth-century Renaissance. Features of particular interest include a marvellous set of choir stalls and a number of paintings from the Venetian school. There are two fine reliefs, one of the apostle Paul and the other of the scourging of Christ. Among the valuable items in the treasury are a sixteenth-century bishop's crosier. This masterpiece of the goldsmith's art is covered with biblical figures.

A Franciscan monastery stands on a small promontory to the east of the harbour. Though founded in the fifteenth century, it was rebuilt in the sixteenth following its destruction by the Turks. There is a fine madonna above the west door, and a collection of valuable paintings inside, including the *Last Supper* by Matteo Roselli, a pupil of Veronese. This is on display in the former refectory, which has been converted into a museum. Still standing in the monastery gardens is a massive 400-year-old cypress.

There is a promenade running west along the shore from the boat harbour via a series of small bays. It passes the famous marble swimming baths that were once considered the finest in Dalmatia.

There is a series of small, irregular islands lying off the coast here to the south-west. Known as the **Pakleni Otoci** or Devil's Islands, they are within easy reach by boat. Sveti Klement is the largest, and offers a fine sandy beach. The much smaller island of Jerolim is a nudist colony.

Fortress overlooking Hvar Island

Six kilometres inland from Hvar, the picturesque little village of **Brusje** is surrounded by fields full of rosemary. The road continues to the small port of **Starigrad** (Città Vecchia), which is situated on the north coast, 17km from Hvar and at the end of a long wooded inlet. Once the main town on the island, it is also the site of the ancient Greek colony of Pharos after which the island was named. Features of interest include the remains of the ancient cyclopean masonry, the church in the Dominican friary, and the castle that belonged to the sixteenth-century poet Petar Hektorovic. The church of Sveti Ivan (St John) dates back to the fourteenth century. The hotels and beaches are well outside the old town. There is a regular ferry service from Split*.

Eight kilometres to the east is the lovely little resort of **Vrboska** which is situated at the head of a small inlet. It is popular for its fine beaches surrounded by pinewoods, and for its sixteenth-century fortified church. The more modern parish church of St Laurence contains paintings by Venetian and Yugoslav masters.

Not far from Vrboska is the small port of **Jelsa**. It is a pretty little coastal resort surrounded by parks and pinewoods. The parish church dates back to the sixteenth century. There are many bathing beaches nearby, including Mina, Glavica and Grebisca. Only 15 minutes away by boat, the tiny island of Zecevo is a haven for nudists.

A small side-road goes south from Jelsa to the tiny south-coast village of **Zavala**. Opposite is the small island of **Scedro**, which is only inhabited in the summer. It is covered with a dense layer of bushes, and also includes the ruins of an old monastery.

The main road continues east from Jelsa via a number of small villages, and after 48km arrives at **Sucuraj** at the eastern tip of the island. This small village is situated among the fig trees and olive groves below the ruins of a Venetian fortress. A ferry goes from here to the tiny mainland port of Drvenik.

Koper (Formerly Capodistria)

Istria

Koper is a small port originally built on an island. The Greeks called it Aegidia and the Romans Capris. Nowadays it is still often known by its Italian name Capodistria. It became Venetian in 1279, Austrian in 1813, and in 1918 it became Italian again. It has belonged to Yugoslavia since the end of World War II.

The main square is particularly impressive, and is bounded to the east by the cathedral, built in the fifteenth and sixteenth centuries in the Lombard Gothic style. Its most interesting features are the altarpieces, a painting by Vittore Carpaccio, the carved choir stalls, and the tomb of St Nazarius, the patron saint of the town. Also to the east of the main square is the **Fontico** — a fourteenth-century granary, whose façade is covered with shield decorations. Not far from the cathedral, the church of **Sveta Anna** contains works by Benedetto Carpaccio and Girolama da San Croce, plus an altarpiece that incorporates paintings by Cima da Conegliano.

The fifteenth-century **town hall** stands on the south side of the square. Of particular interest are the outside staircase, the Moorish window arches and the shields and memorials decorating the outside walls. To the south of the square is a seventeenth-century fountain that is built in the form of a Venetian bridge. Not far away is the Muda Gate, built in the sixteenth century.

There is a Venetian Gothic loggia on the north side of the square. The large building to the west is the **Palazzo Tacco**. This lovely old Venetian palace has been turned into a museum showing the history of the town. Further west, next to the harbour, there is a sixteenth-century salt warehouse called the Taverna.

Koper is not exactly a seaside resort, but there is a pebble beach among the rocks at nearby Zusterna that is suitable for bathing.

Visitors are recommended to make an excursion inland to the famous Postojna Caves* (about 60km). There are several places worth visiting on the way to Postojna. They include the ruined castle at **Socerb** (400m (1,312ft), from which there is a magnificent view, and the Trinity Church at **Hrastovlje**, with its late Gothic frescos. Both are only a short way off the main route.

There are some other interesting caves a little further along the route. The **Skocjan Caves** (Skocjanske Jame) are 10km north of Kozina, and can be reached via the villages of Divaca or Matavun. Formerly known as the Sankt Kanzian Caves, they form a vast labyrinth of grottos and waterways. The path is much longer and more difficult than the one through the Postojna Caves, but it provides an exciting walk along the River Reka through vast rocky chasms and past wild foaming rapids.

Korcula Island (Formerly Curzola)

Dalmatian Coast: Central Section

Korcula is the sixth-largest of the islands in the Adriatic. It is 46km long and up to 8km wide, with a total area of 296sq km. It is situated to the south of the island of Hvar*, and to the west of the Peljesac Peninsula*, from which it is divided by a channel only 2km wide. The highest point on the island is the Klupca (568m (1,863ft)). Some parts of the island are very hilly, some covered in forest, and others relatively fertile — hence the fairly dense pattern of settlement. A road runs the whole length of the island, linking the main towns and villages together. There are ferry connections from Split* to Vela Luka and from Orebic on the Peljesac Peninsula* to Korcula. There are further boat services from Rijeka and Dubrovnik.

The island is thought to have been inhabited since prehistoric times. The Greeks founded a colony here, calling the island Corcyra Melaena or 'land of black forests'. When the Romans took over, their own version of the name was Corcyra Nigra. The island was much fought over. In 1298 there was a sea battle here between the Genoese and the Venetians, during which the famous Venetian explorer Marco Polo was captured by the Genoese (some say he was born on Korcula). In 1420 the Venetians gained firm possession of the island, which they called Curzola. From 1797 until 1918, it belonged successively to Austria, France, Russia, France again, Britain, and Austria again. It was then occupied by Italy until 1920, and since then has remained part of Yugoslavia.

Korcula (Curzola) is by no means the largest town on the island, but is the most important from the tourist's point of view. It is situated towards the eastern end of the island, and is served by ferries from Orebic across the channel on the Peljesac Peninsula*. The small town is beautifully situated on a peninsula, surrounded by large parts

of its fifteenth-century towers and ramparts.

The thirteenth-century cathedral of **Sveti Marko** stands at the highest point of the town. The façade is very impressive, and there is a valuable Tintoretto painting inside. The treasury is housed in the abbey adjoining the cathedral. There is a dome on top of the bell tower.

The **Gabrieli Palace** nearby is now the municipal museum, containing valuable Greek and Roman finds. The church of **Svi**

Sveti (All Saints) was built in 1301, and includes a boxed ceiling from 1613. The museum opposite contains a fascinating collection of

icons.

There is a sixteenth-century loggia next to the harbour. The

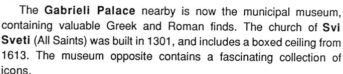

massive land gate dates back to the seventeenth century. Also from the seventeenth century is Leonardo Foscolo's triumphal arch, which stands opposite the sixteenth-century town hall. Korcula still has a

Old Korcula

number of fine old houses that once belonged to the Venetian nobility.

Korcula retains many of its old customs and traditions. The traditional Moreska dance, for example, was once confined to 27 July, but is now performed on most Thursdays between April and October for the benefit of tourists. It is a spectacular sword dance, representing historical events that occurred during the period when the townspeople had to fend off Turkish attacks.

If one goes west out of the old town, one comes to the sixteenth-century Dominican friary of **Sveti Nikola**. A promenade runs east along the shore, passing a swimming pool and a bathing complex. There are further bathing facilities at the nearby beaches of Srcica, Banja and Vrborica.

There are a number of small islands off the coast here, of which the largest is **Badija**. A popular tourist resort with a newly-built sports centre, it also has a Franciscan monastery with fine sixteenth-century cloisters. The smaller island of **Vrnik** is also worth visiting, and is the site of an old Roman quarry.

The village of **Lumbarda** is only a few kilometres away at the south-eastern corner of the island. It has a fine sandy beach, and is

Ancient tower, Korcula

famous for its good local wines, known as Grk.

Blato is the largest town on the island. It is 41km by road from Korcula, and is situated inland in a fertile area near the western end of the island. The chief items of interest are a medieval loggia, a fourteenth-century church and a number of old patricians' houses. Blato is famous for the Kumpanija, a folk festival that takes place here every April; its main attraction is a series of old sword dances performed in traditional costume.

The small port of **Vela Luka** is 7km from Blato on the west coast of the island. It is prettily situated at the head of a 7km-long inlet, and is served by ferries from the mainland port of Split*. Vela Luka is also a major fishing port, including (among other things) a lobster farm. The beach is at some distance from the town, and is surrounded by pinewoods. A new spa is being developed here, involving mud baths that are supposed to cure rheumatism and women's problems. Out in the middle of the bay is the small island of **Osljak**, which has been designated a nature reserve.

Kotor (Formerly Cattaro)

Montenegrin Coast

The small town of Kotor is situated at the head of a long inlet at the end of the Gulf of Kotor, in the shadow of the mighty Lovcen massif. With its well preserved ramparts and defences, it is a remarkable example of a medieval walled city. The present-day population has long since spread out beyond the walls. Kotor was, alas, badly damaged in the great earthquake of 1979.

Kotor

Originally a Roman colony, the town belonged to the Byzantine Empire until 1185, when it became part of the kingdom of Serbia. It was Venetian from 1420 to 1797, while retaining a certain amount of independence. From 1797 to 1814 it changed hands between Britain, France, Russia and Montenegro. Since then it has shared the same history as the rest of the coast.

One enters the old town via the main gate to the west, which was built in 1555. There is parking available in the harbour square immediately in front of it. Next to the main square are the town hall and a clock tower dating back to 1602.

Not far away is the great twelfth-century Roman Catholic cathedral of **Sveti Tripun**. The twin towers are seventeenth-century and the ciborium above the high altar dates from 1352. The reliquary adjoining the treasury contains the earthly remains of the town's patron saint, Sveti Tripun (St Trifon the Martyr). According to legend the townspeople bought their saint from the Venetians in the ninth century.

Also worth seeing are the Serbian Orthodox church of **Sveti Nikola**, which stands a short distance to the north, and the domed Byzantine basilica of **Sveti Luka**, built in 1195. The church of **Sveta Marija** dates back to 1221, and contains a beautiful fifteenth-century crucifix.

The town still retains a number of its old medieval palaces. One of them now houses the **Marine Museum**, where details of this ancient port's great traditions are preserved for posterity. They include one of Europe's oldest guilds, the Sailors' Guild of Kotor. The municipal archives contain documents from the period between the fourteenth and nineteenth centuries.

There is a marvellous view from the **Tvrdjava Sveti Ivan**, a fortress perched high on the hillside above the town. The city's medieval ramparts also climb up the slopes to a height of 260m (853ft); they have a total length of 4km.

Visitors are recommended to come to Kotor on market days (Tuesdays and Thursdays), when people come in from the country wearing their traditional costumes.

One essential trip from Kotor is a tour of the nearby **Lovcen National Park**. The route leaves Kotor to the south along the road to Dub, but after 3km turns left along the Cetinje road. The next 25km

to Bukovica involve a steep climb over the Lovcen or Bukovica Pass
(1,247m (4,090ft)). There are some marvellous views of the Gulf of
Kotor and inland to the 'black mountains' of Montenegro. There are
thirty-eight hairpin bends on the way up — they have been counted!

Immediately below the top of the pass is the small village of
Njegusi, which was the birthplace of Nikola I, the last king of
Montenegro (1910–18). Near **Krstac**, 4km before Njegusi, there is
a right turn along a rough mountain road that runs south around the
Lovcen massif; it eventually improves, and is in some ways easier to
negotiate from Cetinje* at the other end.

Those wishing to climb the highest peak of the massif, the
Stirovnik (1,749m (5,737ft)), should leave this road along a path via
Kuk. The less energetic can turn off along a side-road that climbs one
of the other four main peaks, the Jezerski Vrh (1,657m (5,435ft)). The
end of the road is only half an hour's walk from the summit. Perched
on the top is the mausoleum of the Montenegrin poet prince, Njegos
or Peter II. There is a magnificent panorama of the mountains of
Montenegro, from Lake Scutari in the south-west to the Durmitor
(2,522m (8,272ft)) in the far north.

Krk Island (Formerly Veglio)

Croatian Coast

Krk is the most northerly of the Kvarner Islands, and indeed of the
Yugoslavian islands as a whole. It is also the largest and the widest
of all the islands, having a total area of 409sq km and a maximum
width of 28km. The highest point is the Obsova (569m (1,866ft))
between Punat and Baska.

There were two settlements on the island as early as the Roman
period, and there is evidence that it was inhabited in prehistoric times.
The modern Croat name Krk is derived from the Roman name
Curicum. The history of Krk is as complex and varied as that of the
rest of the coast. But the island appears to have played an important
role in the development of religious language. For the oldest-known
Slav document, written in 1120 in Glagolitic script, was discovered at
Baska in the south of the island.

Krk's population is distributed among a large number of villages

Voz on the Island of Krk

and hamlets. Most of the villages lie in the more fertile regions to the south and west of the island, while the barren east coast presents a steep, rugged, almost theatening profile to the mainland across the channel. One exception on the east coast is the pretty clifftop village Vrbnik. One reason for the barrenness of this coast is the cold bora wind that blows across from the mainland in the winter with incredible force.

The tiny fishing village of **Voz** lies just to the east of the northern tip of Krk. The mainland is only 1km away across the Tihi Channel, which is now spanned by an impressive 1.3km-long bridge. All the local airport traffic has to cross the bridge, as Rijeka Airport is situated at the northern end of Krk between Voz and the west-coast village of Omisalj.

Omisalj is only 4km from Voz, and is the most northerly village on the western side of the island. The old village is perched on a hill 80m (262ft) above the sea, surrounded by woodlands. There is a good view of the new village below, with the Gulf of Rijeka beyond. The parish church with its fine bell tower was originally built in the thirteenth century, but was heavily restored in the sixteenth. There is a fine beach at Pesje near the harbour, and more good bathing in the neighbouring bays. Apart from Rijeka Airport, there is also an oil refinery nearby.

Krk town

Further south along the western shore, the picturesque little fishing village of **Njivice** is again surrounded by woodland. There is a good beach and a modern hotel development, with facilities for nudist bathing. There is also a small lake nearby.

Twelve kilometres south of Omisalj is the village of **Malinska**, which has long been popular as a quiet seaside resort. The village spreads out along the side of the bay. Apart from several small stony bathing beaches, there are two large swimming pools. Further along the coast is the modern holiday village of Haludovo.

The road from Omisalj turns inland at this point, and after 14km arrives at the south coast resort of **Krk** which is the main village on the island. It was originally settled by the Illyrians; they were later replaced by the Greeks and then the Romans, who called the place Curicum. Only recently a number of ancient remains have been discovered here.

The old town has retained many of its original medieval ramparts and towers, together with a twelfth-century Frankopan (Frangipani) castle. The cathedral was also built in the twelfth century; it contains a number of interesting paintings and tombstones. The Franciscan church is also very much worth a visit. The Bay of Drazica stretches out to the east of Krk; there is a good shallow beach and a swimming pool. The small island of **Plavnik** rises up out of the sea to the south-west, though it is actually closer to Cres* than to Krk.

Only 4km east of Krk is the small town of **Punat**. This pleasant bathing resort spreads out along the shore of a broad lagoon that is linked to the sea by a narrow channel. There is a promenade along the shore, and a small shipyard and a marina at the entrance to the lagoon. There are hotels and a swimming pool along the seafront, and a nudist beach somewhat further away. Situated among the vineyards on the north side of the lagoon is the tiny eighth-century church of Sveti Dunat. On the small island of Kosljun in the middle of the lagoon, there is an old Benedictine monastery with a library and some valuable collections.

Sixteen kilometres from Punat and near the island's south-eastern point is the old village of **Baska** which is linked by ferry to the mainland town of Senj*. It lies in a beautiful setting next to a 2km-long beach. The surroundings are very fertile, and the nearby slopes are covered with vineyards, olive groves and fig trees. Baska is famous as the place where the oldest-known document in Glagolitic script was discovered. The original is in the museum at Zagreb, but there is a copy of it in the church of Sveta Lucija in the nearby village of **Jurandvor**. Situated off the south-eastern point of the island is the small uninhabited island of **Prvic**.

Returning across the island towards Punat, there is a side-turning to the east-coast village of **Vrbnik**. This pretty little old village is perched high up on a cliff, 50m (164ft) above the shore. It is full of narrow streets lined by lovely old houses. The fifteenth-century parish church has a sixteenth-century bell tower and a number of valuable paintings. Of particular interest is the library of the Vitezic family, which contains books published in the fifteenth and sixteenth centuries. The newer parts of the village are outside the old town walls. There is a small harbour with a bathing beach on the shore below.

Further north along the east coast, the small fishing village of **Silo** is developing rapidly as a seaside resort. It is served by ferries across the channel from the Croatian Coast resort of Crikvenica.

Vrbnik, on the east coast of Krk

Baska

Kvarner Islands *see* **Cres and Losinj; Krk Island; Rab Island**

Lesina *see* **Hvar Island**

Losinj/Lussigno *see* **Cres and Losinj**

Makarska

Dalmatian Coast: Central Section

The tourist resort of Makarska forms the centre of the so-called Makarska Riviera or Makarska Primorje — a scenic stretch of coastline extending from Omis in the north to Metkovic in the south, or between the rivers Cetina and Neretva. Makarska is a spruce little town. It is built in a semicircle around a small harbour beneath the mighty Biokovo Mountains. The extensive beach faces the open sea along a pleasant stretch of coastline outside the main town. The promenade is lined with rows of palm trees.

This delightful little town has a long and fascinating history. It is

Makarska

believed to have originally been settled by the Phoenicians. During the Roman period it was the port for the nearby town of Mucurum. It was settled by Slavs in the seventh century AD, and was later part of the kingdom of Croatia. It was Turkish for 150 years from the end of the fifteenth century to the middle of the sixteenth, when it was acquired by the Venetians. From then onwards its history was much the same as that of the rest of Dalmatia.

In the main square there is a statue of the poet Andrija Kacic-Miosic (1704–60). Next to it is the eighteenth-century Baroque church of **Sveti Marko**. In the south-eastern part of the town there is an interesting old Franciscan monastery. Its church was used as a mosque during the period of Turkish rule. The library and archives contain some valuable paintings and sculptures, plus a fascinating collection of sea shells.

Holidaymakers in Makarska are recommended to visit the nearby islands of Brac* and Hvar*. There is a ferry from Makarska to Sumartin on the island of Brac. More adventurous visitors are encouraged to climb the nearby peak of **Sveti Jura** (1,762m (5,779ft)), the highest of the Biokovo Mountains. The climb takes 4 hours, and can be extremely tiring in the summer heat. It is therefore advisable to set off very early in the morning.

Mostar

Dalmatian Coast: Central and Southern Sections

The city of Mostar is situated about 65km from the coast in the valley of the River Neretva, and is surrounded by barren karst mountains. It has a population of 110,300, and is the capital of the district of Hercegovina within the constituent republic of Bosnia–Hercegovina. Its situation in the bottom of a steep mountain valley makes it one of the hottest places in Yugoslavia during the summer months.

There is believed to have been a fortified wooden bridge here since Roman times. It was replaced by a stone bridge in the sixteenth century. Originally no more than a small village, Mostar developed into a thriving market town. The old city still retains much of the heritage of centuries of Turkish Moslem rule.

The old town is centred around the **old bridge**, which was built in 1566 by the Turks. It forms a single arch over the Neretva, with a tower at either end. The arch has a span of 29m (95ft) and a maximum height of 20m (66ft). The towers were built in the seventeenth century; one of them was used as a gunpowder store, and the other as a prison and guard chamber.

Mostar has about forty mosques, some of which are still used for Moslem worship. The most interesting of them is the sixteenth-century **Karadzozbeg Mosque**. Another place worth visiting is the bazaar — the old market area on the left bank of the river near the bridge. It includes a number of old buildings from the Turkish period. One of the houses on the bank of the Neretva can be viewed inside

Old Bridge, Mostar

for a small fee. Another place of interest is the famous Street of the
Goldsmiths. The nineteenth-century Eastern Orthodox church contains a number of interesting icons; it provides a fine view of the city,
surrounded by vineyards, orchards and tobacco fields.

There are several interesting places to visit along the route down
to the coast. Twelve kilometres out of Mostar there is a turning for the
Buna Springs. Further on towards Metkovic, the road passes the
lovely little old town of **Pocitelj**. The whole place has a distinctly
oriental flavour, with its medieval castle, its seventeenth-century

Turkish fortifications, the sixteenth-century mosque, the medrese (school of Islam), and a large number of old Turkish houses.

Pag Island (Formerly Pago)

Croatian and Dalmatian Coasts

With an area of 295sq km, Pag is the fifth-largest of the Adriatic islands and the most northerly of the Dalmatian group. It is 59km long, and its width varies between 2km and 10km. It is only very slowly being opened up to tourist traffic. This is mostly on account of the wild, barren terrain and the irregular shape of the island, which is made up of long peninsulas separated by inlets. The highest point is the Sveti Vid (348m (1,141ft)).

The island stretches out parallel to the coast, from which it is divided by the Velebit Channel (Velebitski Kanal), which in places is no more than 2km or 3km wide. The southern tip of the island is separated from the North Dalmatian Coast by a channel only 200m (656ft) wide. A road bridge crosses this channel to nearby Miletici on the mainland; it continues to Posedarje on the main coast road, forming one of the main routes onto the island. There are two ferry routes to Pag: from Jablanac to Stara Novalja in the north, and from Karlobag to the small town of Pag in the centre of the island.

There are the remains of a small Roman colony on the island, near the modern hamlet of Caska. The island was later settled by Croats. The island capital, Pag, was founded in the fifteenth century. The island's population live from fishing, wine and cheese production, and sheep farming. Pag Island is famous for its sheep's cheese (a kind of Parmesan), and for its beautiful lace and embroidery.

The north-western end of the island consists of a long, straight spit of land, the Luna peninsula, at the tip of which is the small village of **Lun**. This is a popular destination for boat trips from the nearby island of Rab* to the north. Its tiny port of Tovarnele is the site of some ancient remains.

The small fishing port of **Novalja** lies at the base of the same peninsula. It is surrounded by vineyards and sheep farms. The shallow beach is lined by pinewoods, and is ideal for children. There are several more good beaches nearby.

Pag

Five kilometres to the north-west of Novalja is the village of **Stara Novalja**. Built on the site of an ancient settlement, it is linked by ferry to the tiny mainland port of Jablanac. The tiny hamlet of **Caska** lies just to the south-east of Novalja at the northern end of a 13km-long gulf. It is near the site of a former Roman colony, which is now flooded, as the island is gradually sinking.

The small town of **Pag** (Pago) is situated in the middle of the island at the southern end of the same gulf, which is linked by a narrow channel to the Velebit Channel. There is a ferry from Pag across the Velebit Channel to Karlobag. The large saltpans nearby produce as much as 15,000 tonnes of salt every year. There is a good beach with as much as 400m of sand. There is also a hotel, a swimming pool and some guesthouse accommodation.

The old town still retains some of its old buildings, together with parts of the old city walls. The old cathedral dates back from the eleventh century and the palace next to it dates back to the fifteenth century. The west door of the cathedral is particularly impressive. There is a school of lacemaking, where local young women learn the delicate art of reticella lacemaking. Women can still often be seen in front of their homes making the famous Pag lace. A folk festival is held in Pag from 26 to 29 July every year.

Next to a salt lake only 3km away are the ruins of the old abandoned city of Starigrad. They include some remains of the old medieval walls and of the fourteenth-century parish church.

Further south there is another curiosity: a freshwater lake called the Velo Blato that is gradually being transformed into a swamp. It is full of birds and fish, especially eels, and is also inhabited by tortoises. The nearby village of **Povljana** on the west coast provides good bathing facilities.

There are several small islands just off the west coast of Pag. The island of **Vir** to the south-west is linked via a bridge to the mainland near the village of Nin. It is fairly barren, but supports a number of villages. It rises to a height of 112m (367ft) above sea level, and has a lighthouse that is visible for some distance around. Further north, the two tiny islands of **Skrda** and **Maun** rise 50m (164ft) from the sea; they are virtually uninhabited.

Peljesac Peninsula

Dalmatian Coast: Central and Southern Sections

The mountainous Peljesac Peninsula is some 70km long, and lies off the Dalmatian Coast opposite the mouth of the Neretva. It is linked to the mainland at the eastern end by a narrow isthmus at Ston. From here it stretches out westwards between the mainland to the north and the islands of Korcula* and Mljet to the south.

The road onto the peninsula leaves the main coast road near Dunta Doli, and after 6km arrives at **Ston**. Ston is made up of the two small villages of Mali Ston and Veliki Ston; they are separated by a ridge, and lie on either side of the isthmus that forms the base of the peninsula. In the fourteenth century Ston was a town of some size belonging to the republic of Ragusa (Dubrovnik). There are still some remains of the old Ragusan defences, including a medieval round tower.

The church of Sveti Mihajlo contains some old Slav frescos from the eleventh century. The Franciscan church also has a fourteenth-century relief depicting St Nicholas. Of the old patricians' houses that remain, the most interesting is the bishop's palace, built in the Renaissance style. The village is famous for its oysters. There is bathing in the nearby inlet, and a somewhat larger beach about 3km away.

The road follows a hilly and often narrow and winding course along the peninsula, with side-turnings to various resorts along either coast. About 33km from Ston, the two villages of **Zuljana** and **Trstenik** lie on either side of a bay on the south coast of the peninsula. Trstenik and the nearby village of Potomje are the home of the famous Dingac wines.

After another 14km there is a turning for **Trpanj** on the north coast of the peninsula, which is linked by ferry to Kardeljevo across the Neretva Channel. Most of the village lies somewhat away from the coast, where there is an extensive shallow beach. There is a ruined fortress on the hill overlooking the village.

The main road continues for another 17km to **Orebic**. The main village on the peninsula lies on the south side of the peninsula opposite the island of Korcula*. There is a ferry service from Orebic to the town of Korcula itself. The village is surrounded by vineyards and groves of orange, lemon and olive trees. The setting is so beautiful that it has become the traditional place for Adriatic sea captains to retire to. Their pretty villas are scattered all along what has become known as the Peljesac Riviera. There are several beaches along the 4km stretch of coastline from Orebic to Trstenica.

Orebic

From time immemorial, Orebic has been the home of seafarers. In the fourteenth century it became part of the republic of Ragusa (Dubrovnik). Shipping expanded enormously from the sixteenth century onwards, and many sea captains accumulated vast fortunes. For centuries, men from around Orebic sailed all over the world under the flags of many different nations.

The Maritime Museum is especially worth visiting. There is also a monastery on a rock called the Gospa od Karmela. In front of it is a stone table overshadowed by tall ancient cypresses. Three kilometres up the hillside is the Franciscan monastery of Sottomonte, whose fifteenth-century church contains a beautiful early medieval crucifix. There is a marvellous view from here too.

The more energetic visitor is recommended to try the 4-hour climb up the mighty Sveti Ilija (961m (3,152ft)), the highest mountain on the peninsula. The view from the summit is magnificent, and on clear days one can see Italy. The mountain's Italian name is Monte Vipera on account of the large number of sand vipers that used to live there; nowadays they are relatively rare.

The main road continues west along the beautifully scenic coastline. Four kilometres from Orebic, the pretty little village of

Kucisce is similarly associated with seafaring. It is followed by
Viganj, where there is a fine Baroque chapel near to an extensive
pebble beach. The road turns inland, and after 8km comes out at the
hamlet of **Lovisce** next to a small bay at the far western end of the
peninsula.

Plitvice Lakes

Croatian Coast

The Plitvice Lakes are probably one of the greatest natural wonders
that Yugoslavia has to offer. There are two routes from the coast. The
first is from Senj* over the Vratnik Pass (72km), and the second from
Karlobag over the Stara Vrata Pass (106km). There is also good
quick access from the inland city of Karlovac.

    The lakes are in thickly wooded surroundings in a valley flanked
by mountains up to 1,300m (4,264ft) high. The whole area around the
Plitvice Lakes, or Plitvicka Jezera, has been designated a national
park. They consist of sixteen lakes ranged in terraces up the valley
and linked by rapids and waterfalls. The total distance between the
highest and the lowest lake is about 8km, and the height difference
is 156m (512ft). The waterfalls and rapids vary in height from 3m
(9.8ft) to 45m (147ft). The colours and shades of the forests are
reflected in the lake surfaces, creating an astonishing medley of tints
from bright green to deep blue. The lakes are also full of fish.

    The village of **Plitvicki Ljeskovac** is situated just below the
highest of the lakes. **Plitvice** itself lies 6km further north next to the
largest lake, Lake Kozjak. There is a camping site by the shore, plus
a number of car parks from which one can easily walk to the visitors'
entrances to the lake enclosures (there is an entry fee). The national
park consists of 20,000 hectares of vast, almost primeval forests,
supporting a rich variety of flora and fauna.

Podgorica *see* **Titograd**

Pola *see* **Pula**

Waterfall, Plitvice National Park

Porec (Formerly Parenzo)

Istria

The small town of Porec forms the central point of the west coast of Istria, both culturally and geographically. It was founded in prehistoric times, and the Romans set up a military camp here. They called it Parentium, and eventually gave it town status. Remains of the former temples of Mars and Neptune can be seen to the north-west of the harbour next to the Riviera Hotel, including a number of columns and sarcophagi.

The most remarkable building in Porec is the triple-naved **Basilica Euphrasiana**. It was built under Bishop Euphrasius in the sixth century AD, and is a beautifully preserved example of a Byzantine church. It is most famous for its remarkable mosaics, with their amazing gold leaf incrustations. The basilica stands on the site of an earlier fifth-century church; some of its mosaic flooring has also been preserved. There is an octagonal font in the forecourt, and the bishop's palace stands next door. Though also built in the sixth century, it has been heavily restored down the centuries. The bell tower dates from the fifteenth century.

Not far from the basilica is the fourteenth-century Gothic church of **Sveti Franjo**. It is unusual in having been converted into a two-storey structure. The upper floor with its Baroque decorations was used as the chapter house. The main street and those adjoining it contain a number of old houses built in the Venetian Gothic and Renaissance styles. One building of particular interest is a Romanesque house with an external staircase. The Sincic Palace contains an interesting museum.

The town itself lies in a beautiful setting, surrounded by green hills. The seafront promenade is very pleasant, and leads to a number of extensive beaches. Opposite the harbour is the tiny island of **Sveti Nikola**, which can be reached via a motorboat shuttle service. It has four hotels, and there are bathing facilities available.

There are numerous beaches either side of Porec. Twelve kilometres up the coast towards Novigrad are the two big holiday villages of Lanterna and Solaris, providing hotel and villa accommodation; Solaris is a nudist colony. There are several more recent

Sveti Nikola

holiday settlements along the coast in between, including Cervar–Porat, Materada–Spadici and Pical; they all provide good facilities for bathing, sports, leisure and entertainment. Going south from Porec, there are the large holiday centres of Brulo, Plava Laguna and Zelena Laguna, and finally the rather smaller settlement of Funtana.

Postojna Caves (Formerly Adelsberg Caves)

Istria and the Croatian Coast

The Postojna Caves, known in Slovene as the Postojanske Jame, are without doubt the most remarkable caves in Europe. The only other caves that could possibly match them are the Castellana Caves in Apulia in south-eastern Italy, which were discovered in 1938.

The caves are situated just outside the pretty little town of **Postojna** (Adelsberg). They are 52km south-west of the Slovenian capital of Ljubljana, 52km east of the Italian border city of Trieste, and 78km north of Rijeka*. Although not close to the Yugoslavian coast, they are nonetheless within easy enough reach for a day trip from many of its resorts. Excursions are organised from towns and resorts all along the coast, from Ankaran near the Italian border to Novi Vinodolski opposite the island of Krk.

These giant caves can only be visited in the company of an expert guide. The temperature remains constant at about 9°C (48°F), so some warm clothing is necessary, especially if it is hot outside. The visit begins with a 3km journey along a narrow gauge electric railway that goes deep into the mountainside; this is followed by 2km on foot through an endless labyrinth of corridors and caverns, and the return ride to the surface by train. Two hours are required to complete this journey of a lifetime through the vast caverns of Postojna.

The route first enters the 110m-long (361ft) 'Great Cathedral'. This is followed by the great 'Dance Hall', 750sq m (2,460sq ft). The 'Crystal Corridor' then leads via the 'Branch Hall' (600sq m (1,968sq ft)) and the 'Crystal Hall' to the great 'Concert Hall', which is the largest cavern of all. Its name is appropriate in that it is sometimes used for such events. Other caves include the 'Winter Hall', the 'Old Grotto' and the impressive 'Calvary Grotto'.

The stalagmites and stalactites display a unique richness of colour and shape. One interesting local curiosity is an animal called the olm — a kind of primitive salamander that is found exclusively in the karst caves of Yugoslavia and northern Italy. Several tame specimens are kept in a pool inside the caves so that visitors can see them.

There are several other interesting things to be seen in the area around Postojna. The first is a castle called the **Predjamski Grad**, which is 10km to the north-west of Postojna. It stands 123m (403ft) up on a rocky outcrop, and is built into a large gap in the rock. This fifteenth-century structure is one of the best-preserved medieval castles in the whole of Slovenia. It contains a large number of archaeological finds from the surrounding area.

Another place worth visiting is the **Cerknisko Jezero**. This lake is about 25km to the east of Postojna, and can be reached via the villages of **Rakek** and **Cerknica**. Although 10km long, it is only filled with water when the rainfall is high. In hot or dry weather the water soaks away through holes in the ground.

Rakek and Cerknica are not far from the **Rak Valley**, which has been designated a national park. The small river runs partly underground, and is spanned in places by natural bridges of rock.

Pula (Formerly Pola)

Istria

Pula is the main cultural and administrative centre of the Istrian Peninsula. Originally no more than an anchorage for the Roman fleet, the port flourished under the emperors and became the great Roman city of Pola. Its importance dwindled in the Middle Ages, but recovered again in the nineteenth century, when the Austrians turned it into a major base for their Adriatic fleet. The naval port, the arsenal and the shipyards all date back to this period.

The town nestles among the hills next to the shore of a well-sheltered bay near the southernmost point of the peninsula. The three islands out in the bay are called Katarina, Andrija and Uljanik. The last of these is linked to the mainland, and forms part of the harbour docklands.

 The ancient amphitheatre is separated from the harbour by no more than an area of parkland. It is 133m (436ft) long by 105m (344ft) wide and 33m (108ft) high. Although built in the first century AD, it is so well preserved that dramas, operas and concerts are still staged here during the summer months.

Many of the most interesting buildings are grouped around the hill on which the castle stands. It was built in the seventeenth century on the site of the former Roman capitol, and there is a commanding view from the top. On the north-eastern side towards the amphitheatre is the Porta Gemina or Twin Gate, which was built in the second century AD. Next to it is the even older Hercules Gate, which still bears some interesting reliefs. Both gates stand close to the **Archaeological** **Museum**, which is full of treasures from the Bronze Age and from the Greek, Roman and Byzantine periods.

At the southern end of the modern main square is a triumphal arch called the **Porta Aurea** or Golden Gate, built by Sergius in 30 BC; it is amazingly well preserved. Going west from here towards the forum, there is a beautiful mosaic in the forecourt of house number 16. It covers an area of 65sq m (213sq ft), and was discovered only a few years ago.

The site of the former Roman forum is now known as the Square of the Republic (Trg Republike). Next to it stands the town hall, which was originally built in the thirteenth century among the remains of the former Roman Temple of Diana; it was later rebuilt in the Renaissance and Baroque styles. The nearby **Temple of Augustus** was built in the first century AD, but is nonetheless remarkably well preserved.

Standing immediately below the western end of the castle hill is the church of **Sveti Franjo** (St Francis). Most of it was built in the early Gothic style, but the west door is thirteenth-century Romanesque. The fifteenth-century cathedral stands further north towards the harbour.

There are several beaches and holiday villages in the bays and inlets either side of Pula, though none bordering the town itself. The best-known are Stoja, Solina and Polstinje, together with the holiday village of Verudela.

Visitors are recommended to make a short trip south via **Premantura** and the pretty little village of **Kamenjak** to the tip of Cape Kamenjak, the most southerly point of the Istrian Peninsula. The whole coast in between is strewn with small pebbly beaches and hotels. North-east across the bay from the cape is the village of **Medulin**, where a large number of hotels have sprung up next to the beach.

There are some important Roman remains near **Vizace**, 12km due east of Pula. Eight kilometres north of Pula, opposite the small fishing village of **Fazana**, there is a group of thirteen tiny offshore islands. The largest of them is called **Brijuni**, though it is much better known by its old Italian name of **Brioni**. This was once the most fashionable seaside resort in the whole of Europe, thanks to its mild climate and lush, subtropical vegetation. It later became President Tito's summer residence.

Rab Island (Formerly Arbe)

Croatian Coast

Rab is the most popular of the Kvarner Islands, indeed of the

Roman amphitheatre, Pula

Yugoslavian islands as a whole. The island looks decidedly inhospitable from the mainland, with a wall of sheer cliffs running the whole length of the east coast. But the west coast is much gentler, consisting of hill slopes covered in woodlands. The climate is mild, with an annual average temperature of 15°C (59°F), favouring the production of good wine, olives, figs and oranges.

The island is 22km long and between 3km and 10km wide. The highest point is to be found in the Kamenjak Vrh, one of the three ranges of steep hills that run from north to south along the island, interspersed by fertile green valleys.

Rab was first settled by the Liburnians, and later by the Greeks and Romans. The Phoenicians, however, are believed to have founded a colony here first. The Croats settled here during the seventh century AD, since when the island has shared much the same history as the rest of the islands nearby. The Romans called the island Arba or Arbe, and the latter was its name during the heyday of Venetian rule.

The beautiful little town of **Rab** (Arbe) is the island's main commercial and tourist centre. It is situated half-way along the west coast on the site of a former Roman settlement. The old town is perched on a promontory, and is partly surrounded by walls. The most distinctive feature of the skyline is the four bell towers, one of which is the finest of its kind along the whole of the coast. The port has boat links with Rijeka* and Zadar*, but the main ferry ports are elsewhere at Pudarica and Lopar (see below).

Next to the main harbour square are the thirteenth-century **Prince's Palace** and the town hall. The harbour gate leads through the sixteenth-century loggia, with its lovely old columns. One can walk up the main street (Ulica Ive Lole-Ribara) past the fourteenth-century **Nimira Palace**, with its beautiful entrance door, and a host of other churches and palaces, whose fine doors and façades bear witness to the town's illustrious past.

A flight of steps leads up from the market square to another street called the Ulica Rade Koncara. Here one can find the small sixteenth-century chapel of **Sveti Kriz** (St Cross), and next to it the remains of the eleventh-century church of **Sveti Ivan** (St John); its Romanesque clock tower is still intact. A small alleyway leads through to the **Komrcar Park**, which is well known for its fine shaded walkways.

Cathedral, Rab

Next to a small square called the Trg Slobode is the sixteenth-century church of **Sveta Justina**, which contains an altarpiece by a pupil of Titian. The nearby Benedictine convent includes the eleventh-century triple-naved church of **Sveti Andrija** (St Andrew); the west door is Renaissance, and the treasures inside include a fine Baroque altar and a painting by Bartolomeo Vivarini in 1485.

The twelfth-century cathedral of Sveta Marija stands next to the cathedral square. The west door is fifteenth-century Renaissance, and includes a *pietà* by a local artist. The main items of interest inside are the beautifully carved choir stalls dating from 1445, and a silver-encrusted shrine containing the relics of St Christopher (Sveti Kristofor), the patron saint of the town. The Romanesque bell tower is a short distance from the cathedral itself. It is 25m (82ft) high, and was built between the twelfth and thirteenth centuries. Visitors may climb to the top, from which there is a fine view of the town and its surroundings.

Out on the point beyond the cathedral is the fifteenth-century convent of St Antony; there is a statue of the saint at the west door. There is a pleasant footpath along the west shore of the promontory below the cathedral and the Komrcar Park. About an hour's walk along this is the Franciscan monastery of S**veta Eufemija**, which was also built in the fifteenth century. The cloisters are particularly fine, and the church contains some valuable paintings by artists such as the brothers Vivarini.

The wooded area behind the monastery is the **Dundo Forest**, which can also be reached via a direct route from the town. It is one of the most beautiful forests on the whole coast, with a rich variety of trees, including pines, cypresses, oaks and cork oaks; sometimes there is a dense, impenetrable mass of undergrowth. The nearby **Kamenjak** (408m (1,338ft)), the highest point on the island, is only 2 hours' climb on foot from Rab. There is an impressive panorama from the top.

The bathing is good on the shore below the Komrcar Park, and there are several other good bathing beaches nearby, including Banjol, Sveta Eufemija, Padova and the Kalifront Peninsula. Five kilometres out to the west, the holiday village of **Suha Punta** provides ample hotel and villa accommodation, plus a nudist beach in the vicinity.

Six kilometres south-east along the coast from Rab is the small fishing village of **Barbat**, which is popular among gourmets for its good wines and delicious fish dishes (including lobster). It also has a bathing beach in beautiful surroundings. Across a narrow channel is the long, thin island of **Dolin**, which although uninhabited provides good opportunties for bathing.

Further south along the coast, towards the south-eastern tip of the island, the small port of **Pudarica** is linked by a regular ferry service to the mainland village of Jablanac.

Another place worth visiting from Rab is the small village of **Supetarska Draga**, which lies 6km to the north at the head of an inlet. It has a lovely old church and a fine beach in a beautiful setting. Another 6km further on is the larger village of **Lopar**, which is

Rab Island

situated at the head of another inlet on the north side of the island.

Lopar is famous as the birthplace of Marinus, founder of the Republic of San Marino next to the Italian Adriatic Coast, which has remained independent to this day. The bathing at Lopar is particularly good, with 300m of shallow sandy beach. There are ferries from here to Senj* on the mainland and Baska on the island of Krk*.

The road continues to the holiday village of **San Marino**, which is situated next to the Crnika Bay at the northern end of the east coast. The beach is again shallow and therefore suited to children and non-swimmers. The two small islands lying between here and the mainland are **Goli** and **Sveti Grgur**, neither of which is inhabited.

Ragusa *see* Dubrovnik

Rijeka (Formerly Fiume)

Croatian Coast

Rijeka is Yugoslavia's largest port, with a population of 193,000. Vast numbers of tourists pass through here on their way to holiday centres along the coast, but it is usually no more than a port of call, whether for boat, rail or road travellers. The nearby suburb of Susak across the Rijecina is admittedly quieter and more pleasant, but visitors are not generally recommended to stay in this busy industrial city. On the other hand, there is plenty to see here for those passing through.

The first settlement here was the Roman fort of Tarsatica on the nearby hill-top site known today as Trsat. The name Rijeka was first recorded in the thirteenth century, when a small settlement on the right bank of the Rijecina began to grow and flourish. The name Rijeka, like its Italian equivalent Fiume, simply means 'river', and no doubt refers to the river on which it is situated — the Rijecina or 'little river'.

During the centuries which followed, the city changed hands between various noble families, including the famous Frankopans or Frangipanis. In the fifteenth century the Hapsburgs took over the city. In the seventeenth century it became a free port, and gained considerable independence while at the same time acknowledging its allegiance to both Croatia and Hungary.

In 1919 the city was seized by Gabriele d'Annunzio, and came under Italian occupation. However, the new state of Yugoslavia retained the suburb of Susak on the east bank of the Rijecina, and was thus able to use at least part of the port. After World War II the

Rijeka

rest of the city came to Yugoslavia, together with most of the Istrian Peninsula.

The approach road from Opatije provides a good general view of this lively city with its busy port. The first important square that one comes to is the Trg Zabuca, on the north side of which is the nineteenth-century **Capuchin Church**. The south side of the square opens out onto the quay, while the building on the east side is the harbour office. The next square to the east is the Narodni Trg, next to which are the **Jadran Palace** and a modern skyscraper. This is followed by the Trg Republike, at the north end of which are the Library of Science and the **Gallery of the Visual Arts** (Galerija Savremene Umetnosti).

If one continues north from here along the Ulica Supilova, one eventually comes to the **National Museum** (Prirodnjacki Muzej), surrounded by the Vladimir Nazor Park. Formerly the Governor's Palace, this building was also used by Gabriele d'Annunzio. Much of the material contained here has maritime associations. The nearby Natural History Museum includes a small aquarium and a zoo. Further north, in the suburb of Kozala, there is a cemetery with a church, where visitors may climb the tower and get a view of the city.

If one goes east from the Trg Republike along the Korzo Narodne Revolucje, one quickly finds the fifteenth-century City Tower (Gradska Kula) on the left, guarding the old city to the north. The **Roman triumphal arch** next to the old market place is the oldest surviving structure in Rijeka. Immediately to the north is the seventeenth-century church of **Sveti Vid**, with its beautiful Baroque interior, modelled on the church of Santa Maria della Salute in Venice. To the east of the old city is the twelfth-century cathedral of Sveta Marija; though the oldest church building in Rijeka, it has been heavily restored in subsequent centuries.

If one goes south from the old town across the Korzo Narodne Revolucje, one soon comes to the market hall next to the Ulica Ivana Zajce. This is not far from the entrance to the theatre, built in the last century. Behind the theatre is the Mrtivi Kanal (Dead Canal), formerly an arm of the Rijecina. Turning north again along the canal, one comes via the Beogradski Trg to the Titov Trg. This square was built over the Rijecina after World War II on the site of the former border bridge between Italian-occupied Fiume and Susak. Not surprisingly, there is a memorial to the liberation of 1945.

The suburb of **Susak** includes the fascinating hill-top site of **Trsat**, where the Romans first built a fort. It can be reached from the

Titov Trg on foot via a flight of 559 steps, or else along a pleasant road up the hillside. Buildings of interest include a Franciscan monastery with a particularly fine set of cloisters, and a pilgrimage church dedicated to Our Lady of Trsat. The latter was built in the fifteenth century by the Frankopan (Frangipani) princes. According to legend, the Holy House of Nazareth is supposed to have stood here in the thirteenth century before being moved by angels to its present site at San Loreto in Italy. The church contains some lovely fourteenth-century icons painted on cedarwood, and several other interesting paintings and tombstones.

The nearby **Trsat Castle** was the former seat of the Frankopan princes. A small building on the site contains the ethnographic and historical section of the National Museum. Next to it is the thirteenth-century church of **Sveti Jurje**. There are some splendid views, both from the castle tower and from the municipal park that stretches out across the hill to the east.

There are plenty of possible excursions from Rijeka, including the nearby islands of Cres* and Krk* (there is a ferry from Rijeka to Porozina at the northern end of Cres). The famous Postojna Caves* are also within fairly easy reach (78km). Somewhat nearer at hand, the plateau region around **Platak** (24km) lies at 1,111m (3,644ft) above sea level, and provides skiing until well into the spring.

Rovinj (Formerly Rovigno)

Istria

This beautiful little town was originally founded by the Romans, who called it Rovignum. It was a major port for centuries as the chief commercial centre of Istria. However, the population today numbers no more than a few thousand.

The old town of Rovinj is situated on a peninsula that was an island until it was united with the mainland in the eighteenth century. It is extremely picturesque, with its narrow streets and old buildings overlooking the harbour to the south. The Venetian architecture gives the town a distinctly Mediterranean feel, and a beauty that attracts artists here from all over Europe.

The remains of the old walls include three well preserved city

Rovinj

gates. The Baroque town hall and the nearby municipal museum are especially worth visiting. The town is dominated by the great cathedral of **Sveta Eufemija**, built in the eighteenth century. Inside is the tomb of St Euphemia herself, the patron saint of the town, who is also depicted in the weather vane at the top of the tower. The twelfth-century Trinity Chapel is somewhat outside the old town.

The coastal scenery is further enhanced by a group of thirteen tiny offshore islands. The two largest of these are **Katarina** and **Crveni Otok**, both of which provide bathing facilities and hotel accommodation. There are numerous hotel and holiday beaches along the coast on either side of the town. They provide all kinds of facilities for bathing, sports, leisure and entertainment. The two nudist colonies of Monsena and Valalta are both situated to the north-west of Rovinj.

Within easy walking distance to the south is the nature reserve of **Zlatni Rat**. This long peninsula between two bays is famous for its unusual subtropical flora.

Salona *see* **Solin**

Sarajevo

Dalmatian Coast: Central and Southern Sections

Sarajevo (population 500,000) is the capital of the constituent republic of Bosnia–Hercegovina. It is situated in the valley of the Miljacka about 200km from the coast. But in spite of the distance, it is well worth the effort of a visit for those who are able. The city reveals a unique and delightful mixture of east and west, old and new, Turkish and modern Slav. The great influence that the Turks had on the city remains clearly visible to this day.

Without doubt the most fascinating part of the city is the old bazaar, with its narrow streets lined with stalls and craftsmen's workshops. There are all kinds of things for sale — leatherware and shoes; copperware and silverware, including fine filigree work; linen cloth sewn with fine gold and silver thread — just to name but a few of the items available. The narrow streets are full of bustle and life, and on market days one may be lucky enough to see people from the countryside wearing their oriental-looking traditional dress. It is almost as if one had been suddenly lifted out of Europe and dropped down in the orient.

Next to the bazaar is the great **Begova Dzamija** or Husrev-Beg Mosque. Built in the sixteenth century, it is one of the finest mosques in the whole of Yugoslavia. The forecourt contains a covered fountain where worshippers may perform ritual washing before entering the mosque. Next to the mosque is the tomb of Husrev-Beg, probably the most influential city governor in the history of Sarajevo. Opposite the mosque is the Kursumli Medrese, an old Moslem religious school.

To the north of the bazaar is the old Serbian Orthodox church, with the **City Museum** beyond it. A wide street called the Obala Marsala Tita runs west from the old church alongside the municipal park. It passes the lovely sixteenth-century **Ali Pasa Mosque**, and comes out at the **Provincial Museum**, with its fascinating historical, cultural and scientific collections. Next to it is a Bogomil cemetery with some fine tombstones (*stecci*).

The town hall is not far from the bazaar on the bank of the Miljacka. It was built at the end of the last century in a style based on Moorish and Byzantine architecture. It houses the National Library and Art Gallery. To the west of the town hall, next to the **Princip**

Sarajevo

✳ **Bridge,** is the spot where a student called Princip assassinated Archduke Franz Ferdinand of Austria and his consort on 28 June 1914 — the event that precipitated the outbreak of World War I. The place is marked by the student's footprints in the pavement.

The upper town to the east is still mostly Moslem. It is dominated by the castle, which can be entered via the Ploca Gate. There are some marvellous views of the city from the top of the battlements. Across the river is the great sixteenth-century **Imperial Mosque**. The old carpet mill next to the nearby Trg 6 April (Square of the 6 April) is open to the public.

Sebenico *see* **Sibenik**

Senj

Croatian Coast

The small town of Senj is in a wild setting among the barren karst mountains of the Velebit range. There is little vegetation to moderate the force of the bora, which blows stronger here than anywhere else on the coast. It is mercifully rare in the summer.

The town was founded at least as early as the Roman period, and probably even earlier, in the fifth century BC. In the twelfth century it was destroyed and taken over by the Frankopan (Frangipani) princes. In the sixteenth century it was occupied by a band of refugee pirates known as the Uskoks. There followed the most turbulent period in the town's history, during which the Uskoks waged war against both the Turks and the Venetians. They were finally overcome in 1617, when the Treaty of Madrid provided for their resettlement in the Croatian hinterland. The Uskok graves can still be seen, having been rescued from the Franciscan church when it was destroyed during World War II.

The small town is still surrounded by some of its old fortifications. Some of the old houses still have shields and inscriptions providing information about their former owners. The main square or Trg Marka Balena is particularly interesting, being surrounded by old Baroque buildings. The triple-naved Romanesque cathedral dates back to the twelfth century. Senj was also the site of the first Croatian printing press in 1493.

Outside the town, the Eastern Orthodox church of **Sveta Marija** is a place of pilgrimage for sailors. On a hill above the town is the famous sixteenth-century Uskok pirate fortress, known as **Nehaj** or 'fear nothing'; it is still in a fairly good state of repair. There is a bathing beach just to the south of the town.

Senj is well placed for visiting the nearby coast and islands. There are ferries from here to Baska on the island of Krk* and to Lopar on the island of Rab*. A road goes inland over the Vratnik Pass to the beautiful Plitvice Lakes* (72km).

Sibenik (Formerly Sebenico)

Dalmatian Coast: Northern Section

Sibenik is one of the larger towns on the Dalmatian Coast. It is built in terraces on a hill slope overlooking an extensive harbour. The harbour is linked to the sea via the fjord-like Sveti Ante Channel, and is one of the best natural harbours in the whole of the Mediterranean. The view of Sibenik, whether from an approaching ship or from the road viaduct to the north, is possibly one of the most impressive on the whole coast.

The city was founded by the Croats in the tenth century, and by the eleventh century it was the seat of the Croatian kings. Its period of greatest prosperity was under King Kresimir. In the thirteenth and fourteenth centuries there were short periods of Venetian and Byzantine rule. But from 1412 until 1797 it belonged permanently to Venice, despite repeated Turkish attacks. It flourished again towards the end of the Middle Ages, when most of the finest buildings were erected. A large number of great artists and scientists lived here during that period.

The great domed cathedral is by far the most impressive structure in Sibenik. It is only a short distance from the quay, from which it can be reached via a long flight of steps. It was begun in the fifteenth century in the Venetian Gothic style, and is the greatest masterpiece of the famous architect Juraj Dalmatinac. But he did not finish it, and it was completed in the sixteenth century by Niccolo Fiorentino in the style of the early Renaissance. Fiorentino was also responsible for the great 32m-high (105ft) dome.

The central part of the west front is richly decorated with carvings

Sibenik Cathedral

depicting the Apostles being sent out into the world. It is guarded by two stone lions on either side, carrying statues of Adam and Eve to represent the beginning of mankind. The frieze running around the apse includes seventy-two different human sculptures. The barrel-shaped roof is particularly interesting from the inside, as the vaulting is made up of wedge-shaped stone slabs laid on top of one another without any further means of support. To the right of the choir is a richly decorated baptistry. The leaves on the capitals have been so delicately carved that they each give a different note when struck.

The loggia next to the town hall opposite the cathedral was built by Sanmicheli in 1542, and was in fact the original town hall. If one carries on upwards to the left of the town hall, there is a series of steps and alleyways leading past several mansions and small palaces. One eventually comes out into the cemetery below the old **Sveta Ana Fort**, once the town's main defence; and there is a marvellous view of the city and the harbour.

Also worth seeing is the fifteenth-century church of **Sveti Ivan**, which has an open-air staircase by Pribaslavic and a balustrade by Niccolo Fiorentino. The bell tower standing next to it dates from the seventeenth century. To the north of it is the church of **Sveta Marija**, which has a series of seventeenth-century frescos.

The Eastern Orthodox church once belonged to a Benedictine monastery; it has a sixteenth-century bell tower and a fascinating collection of icons. The fourteenth-century church of **Sveti Franjo** has some interesting Renaissance and Baroque altars. The church in the Dominican friary contains two paintings by the younger Palma, while the church of **Sveti Lovre** houses works by painters from the Venetian school.

If one climbs up through the suburb of **Subicevac**, one eventually arrives at the Subicevac Fort, from which there is a wonderful view. A kilometre further to the north-west is the highest fort of all, **Sveti Ivan**.

The other old Venetian fort, **Sveti Nikola**, is on an island in the Sveti Ante Channel that forms the entrance to the harbour. Opposite Sveti Nikola is the beach of **Jadrija**, which is surrounded by pinewoods. The other local beach is **Solaris**, which is 5km out of Sibenik opposite the island of Zlarin. The fine pebble beach is lined with concrete, with a colony of hotels occupying the area behind.

Sibenik

There is much to see among the numerous islands bordering the coast to the west (see the Dalmatian Islands*), many of which can be reached by boat from Sibenik. A trip around the beautiful Kornat Archipelago is especially recommended. The island of Murter is accessible via a bridge from the mainland; the road leaves the main coast road 25km to the north. The magnificent **Krka Falls** (Krka Slap) are particularly worth visiting from Sibenik. The lower falls are probably the most impressive; they are 3km up-river from Skradin (see below) and 15km from Sibenik. The River Krka is 100m (328ft) wide here, and plunges a total of 45m (147ft) in five stages. The noise can be heard for miles around. Above these falls the river has been dammed back to form a long reservoir. One can continue by boat to the island monastery of **Visovac**, which has an old library. The upper falls are at the northern end of the reservoir.

The village of **Skradin** is one of the oldest settlements in Dalmatia. It is 19km by road from Sibenik, but can also be reached by boat along the lower course of the Krka. Its church contains a fascinating icon collection. Skradin was founded by the Liburnians, and was of major importance during the Roman period. There are further Roman remains near Bribir and Benkovac on the road from here to Biograd*.

The village of **Kistanje** is 34km along the road north of Skradin. Five kilometres to the north of it are the remains of the old Roman settlement of Burnum, which was also founded by the Liburnians. To the south of the village is the Eastern Orthodox monastery of **Sveti Arhandjel**, which has a valuable collection of treasures. It looks down onto the Krka at the point where it plunges over the 15m-high (49ft) **Roski Falls**. Eight kilometres east of Kistanje towards Knin is the fourth and highest of the Krka waterfalls, the **Manojlovac Falls**, where the river plunges a total of 60m (197ft) in several stages.

Knin is 21km east of Kistanje and 56km north-east of Sibenik (along a more direct route). This little market town lies in a delightful setting below an old castle. There are records of Knin from as early as the tenth century, and it later became the residence of the kings of Croatia. The old Franciscan monastery houses a museum with a valuable collection of ancient finds. The castle is worth visiting, if only for the marvellous view. Traditional dress is still worn on market days and religious festivals, both in Knin and in the countryside around.

Ruins at Solin

Five kilometres east of Knin, on the road to Vrlika, there is a turning for the Krcic Valley, with the **Krcic Gorge**, and a 22m-high (72ft) waterfall called the **Topoljski Slap**. The road from Vrlika continues south to meet the coast near Split*.

Solin (Formerly Salona)

Dalmatian Coast: Central Section

The small town of Solin lies at the eastern end of the Kastelanski Riviera (Bay of Seven Castles) and 6km to the north of Split*, of which it is effectively an industrial suburb. Immediately to the north, the extensive remains of the great Roman city of **Salona** provide a fascinating excursion into the past.

Salona was originally an Illyrian settlement, and is mentioned in records dating back to 119 BC. In the first century AD, Emperor Augustus made it the capital of the Roman province of Illyricum, and it grew into a flourishing port. Salona was the birthplace of Emperor Diocletian in AD 245. It became a bishopric in the third century AD, and retained its importance after the fall of the Roman Empire. But the city was hard-pressed during the later barbarian invasions, and in AD 614 it was finally destroyed by the Avars.

Excavations have revealed only the foundations of the buildings, but it is still a fascinating place to visit. The amphitheatre, which originally seated 20,000 people, is still clearly recognisable. It is situated just inside the north-western corner of the old city walls. Within these walls are the foundations of houses, baths, a small temple and a Roman theatre.

Outside the walls is the great Roman cemetery or Hortus Metrodori. To the east are the Porta Suburbia and the Porta Caesarea, while the fifth-century Basilica Urbana lies further north next to a small baptistry. The site also includes the foundations of several much older churches. The nearby thermal baths are particularly interesting, and parts of them are remarkably well preserved.

An avenue of cypresses leads away from the city walls to a monument commemorating the archaeologist Bulic, who directed the excavations here for almost half a century. Further north are the remains of the early Christian cemetery of **Monastirine,** next to the ruins of a triple-naved basilica. The inscriptions are still legible on some of the tombstones. Most of the sarcophagi have been broken open.

Split (Formerly Spalato)

Dalmatian Coast: Central Section

With a population of 236,000, Split is the biggest city on the whole of the Yugoslavian coast. Situated mid-way along the coast between Rijeka and Ulcinj, it has grown into a major industrial city. It is Yugoslavia's second most important freight and passenger port (after Rijeka). The railway station is served by trains and carriages from all over Europe, and there is an international airport across the bay to the west.

Split began as a small fishing village with the Greek name Asphalatos. At first it was very much overshadowed by its much larger neighbour, the provincial capital of Salona, only 6km to the north. But the situation changed when Emperor Diocletian (AD 294–305) built a palace here for his retirement. When Salona was destroyed by the Avars in the seventh century AD, some of the people sought refuge within the walls of the great palace, which quickly became the centre of a new and flourishing city.

This city became a bishopric in the eighth century, and eventually passed from the Byzantine Empire into the new kingdom of Croatia. Like the rest of Dalmatia, it came for a short period under Hungarian rule; then in 1420 the Venetians took over for nearly four centuries. It belonged to Austria from 1797 to 1918, apart from a short time during the Napoleonic Wars. Since World War I it has been part of the state of Yugoslavia.

The city is situated on a peninsula that juts out towards the island of Ciovo. Its most dominant geographical feature is a steep hill called the Marjan (178m (584ft)) on the south side of the peninsula. It is 45 minutes' walk from the city, and provides a magnificent view of the town with the mountains behind and the numerous islands out to sea. Across the bay to the north, the Kastelanski Riviera huddles beneath the mighty Kozjak Mountains (780m (2,558ft)), which are divided by a pass from the even higher Mosor Mountains (1,330m (4,362ft)) to the east.

The **Palace of Diocletian** (Dioklecijanova Palaca) still forms the heart of the old city of Split. It is a vast site, measuring 215m (705ft) on the east and west sides, 175m (574ft) to the north, and 179m (587ft) on the south side bordering the sea. Much remains of the original perimeter walls, including three of the four corner towers. The south-west tower facing the harbour has gone, but the north-east tower has been turned into a restaurant, and can be recommended for the marvellous view. Other structures that remain are the Golden, Silver, Iron and Bronze Gates, the peristyle, the mausoleum that later became the cathedral, and the temple of Jupiter that later became the baptistry.

The palace was deserted in 615, when the people of Salona fled here from the Avars. They then built a new fortified city within the walls of the palace. About 3,000 people still live in the 250 houses that remain within the palace precincts. There are houses from all periods of the city's history, all built in the style of their times. The result is a kind of open-air museum of architecture down the centuries.

A few years ago, archaeological experts began to clear out the old cellar vaults of the Roman palace, which had become filled with the rubbish of centuries. They found that the vaulting corresponded with the foundations of old buildings above them that had long since been destroyed — and thus gained some marvellous insights into the building methods of the times. The reliefs and frescos that they unearthed are now on view to the public.

One enters the palace site from the harbour promenade or Titova Obala via the Porta Aenea (Bronzana Vrata or Bronze Gate), which was once directly next to the sea. A narrow street leads through to the cathedral via the old Roman peristyle. Among the old Corinthian columns that once lined the antechamber, there is an ancient Egyptian sphinx that once guarded the entrance to the mausoleum. It is carved out of black granite, and is probably about 3,500 years old.

Diocletian's mausoleum has fortunately been preserved as the cathedral, which was consecrated in the ninth century and dedicated to the Virgin Mary. The main structure is octagonal on the outside and round on the inside. The wooden entrance door is beautifully carved with scenes from the life of Christ. These date from 1214, and are the work of a native sculptor called Buvina. The building is supported on the inside by granite pillars topped by Corinthian capitals, with surrounding columns of red porphyry. The friezes around the walls between the columns depict hunting scenes and portraits of the Roman emperor and his consort. Other interesting features include a fine late Gothic altar, a pulpit mounted on columns, and the richly

Split

carved wooden choir stalls. A Romanesque bell tower was added in the thirteenth century. It was restored at the end of the nineteenth century, and is one of the finest bell towers in Dalmatia. It is 61m (200ft) high, and there is a beautiful view from the top.

The baptistry opposite the cathedral was originally a temple of Jupiter. It is characterised by Corinthian columns, tunnel vaulting and a beautiful boxed ceiling. The entrance door is richly decorated with carvings. The same is true of the stone slabs that form the font, where there is an eleventh-century stone relief of the king of Croatia.

To the east of the cathedral is the Porta Argentea (Srebrna Vrata or Silver Gate), which formed the eastern entrance to the palace. It was not uncovered until the end of World War II. Immediately outside the walls here is the thirteenth-century church of **Sveti Dominik**, which contains a beautiful Baroque altar.

A street called the Dioklecijanova Ulica runs north from the peristyle past the Palazzo Ivelio. To the right of it along the Papaliceva Ulica is the famous **Papaliceva Palaca**. This late Gothic palace built by Juraj Dalmatinac now houses the municipal museum. The Dioklecijanova Ulica carries on north through the Porta Aurea

(Zlanta Vrata or Golden Gate). The northern palace entrance is probably the best-preserved of all the gates, with the ancient city battlements stretching out on either side. The walls are so thick that a small ninth-century chapel has been accommodated in the space between them; it includes a particularly fine stone choir screen.

The small park just to the north of the city walls contains the ruins of the medieval church of **Sveta Eufemija**, plus another small chapel built by Juraj Dalmatinac in the fifteenth century. Immediately in front of the Porta Aurea is an example of modern Yugoslavian art: a sculpture by Mestrovic of Bishop Grgur, who campaigned for the use of Croat as a religious language.

The Kresimirova Ulica goes west from the peristyle past the Cindro Palace to the Porta Ferrea (Gvozdena Vrata or Iron Gate). The small church next to it possesses the oldest tower in the city. The square immediately outside is the Narodni Trg or People's Square, on the other side of which is the old town hall, built in the fifteenth century. This now contains the **Museum of Ethnography**, with fine collections of costumes, embroidery and other local handicrafts. Other buildings around the square include a Romanesque clock tower and the fifteenth-century **Palaca Cambi**.

The next square to the south is the Trg Preporoda. Immediately next to it is the seventeenth-century **Palaca Milesi**, which now houses the Maritime Museum. The nearby Hrvojeva Kula is one of the towers remaining from the city's medieval walls. There is also a simple statue of the poet Marko Marulic.

It is only a few more yards to the harbour promenade or Titova Obala, at the western end of which is a square surrounded by arcades called the Trg Republika. There is a large fountain in the square, and behind it to the left is a Franciscan monastery with a small cloister. The church contains a number of tombs, including that of the poet Marko Marulic.

A road goes south-west along the shore to the suburb of Labud, where there is a beach. Above here on the slopes of the Marjan is the Institute for Oceanography and Fisheries, which includes an aquarium. The road continues past another beach at Zvoncac, and eventually arrives at the **Mestrovic Museum**. Formerly the summer residence of this famous Croat sculptor, it still contains a large number of his works.

Modern harbour, Split

If one goes north from the Trg Republika, one quickly comes to the theatre. Further north along the Zrinjsko-Frankopanska Ulica is the **Archaeological Museum**, with valuable collections of prehistoric, Roman and medieval remains from all over Dalmatia, but chiefly from nearby Salona.

Just to the north of the museum there is a turning for Poljud, where there is a beach and a Franciscan monastery. Though it is first mentioned in the eleventh century, its present structure dates from the fifteenth. In the church there are paintings by Girolama di Santa Croce and other Renaissance artists, while the cloisters contain some fine tombstones.

On a hill to the east of Diocletian's Palace is the seventeenth-century Kastel Gripe. There are several good bathing beaches around the fringes of the city, some of which have been mentioned already. Split is also a spa town, possessing both iodine and sulphur baths.

There is yet more on offer apart from bathing and sightseeing. For Split is also a major cultural centre. The Summer Festival includes a vast programme of drama, opera and concerts. It is no wonder, therefore, that a town like Split, though industrial, is such a popular destination for tourists.

Split is also an ideal centre from which to visit the Dalmatian Islands*. In particular, there are ferries to Rogac on the island of Solta, Vela Luka on Korcula*, Supetar on Brac*, and Vira and Starigrad on the island of Hvar*. But there are many other services to islands and ports along the coast, and even across the Adriatic to the Italian city of Pescara.

Six kilometres to the north, next to the suburb of Solin*, are the remains of the great Roman provincial capital of Salona, where Diocletian was born in AD 245. Solin is also at the eastern end of the famous **Kastelanski Riviera**, with its many castles. The hinterland to the east once belonged to the so-called Peasants' Republic or Free State of Poljica. Both these areas are included in the description of the Dalmatian Coast (see page 69).

A road goes north-east from Solin to the small village of **Klis** (Clissa), situated in the narrow gap between the Kozjak and Mosor Mountains. It is only 14km from Split, and is well worth a visit. The castle on the hillside above the village (360m (1,180ft)) played a vital role in the history of Croatia. It later formed a vital bulwark for the Venetians against the Turks, who captured it in the sixteenth century, only to lose it again to Venice in the seventeenth. Its commanding position made it strategically important even during World War II. There is naturally a good view from the top.

The road carries on inland for another 22km to **Sinj**. This pretty little town is in fertile surroundings, and is also linked to Split by a light railway that comes up through the mountains at Klis. The Baroque church is especially worth a visit, while the Franciscan monastery contains a valuable collection of Roman finds. Sinj is also famous for the Alka Festival in August, celebrating the defeat of the Turks in

1715. The battle is represented by means of ceremonial games on horseback, in which riders and shield-bearers are dressed up in magnificent armour.

The road continues north-west past a long lake called the Perucko Jezero, and eventually arrives at **Vrlika**. Vrlika is well known for its folk dancing, which the people perform in colourful costumes. It is also not far from the source of the Cetina. The road continues to Knin in the valley of the Krka, from which one can return to the coast at Sibenik*.

Titograd (Formerly Podgorica)

Montenegrin Coast

The city of Titograd lies in the middle of a broad plain at the confluence of two rivers. It is the modern capital of Montenegro, and with a population of 132,000 is the smallest capital of a Yugoslavian constituent republic.

The city of Podgorica was first mentioned in about 1200 as the birthplace of Stefan Nemanja, founder of the Serb dynasty of the Nemanjici. It was called Podgorica until the end of World War II, by which time most of the town had been destroyed. A modern city has since grown up from the ruins.

A small portion of the old town has survived on the left bank of the river at **Ribnica**. There is a clock tower called the Sahat Kula, together with the remains of a castle and some relics of an old Roman aqueduct.

It is 47km from Titograd to the old Montenegrin capital of Cetinje*. The road goes through some beautiful scenery via the village of Rijeka-Crnojevica below the ruins of the Obod Monastery and next to an old Turkish stone bridge.

Titograd is only 57km from the sea. The road goes through Virpazar on Lake Scutari, and eventually reaches the coast next to Petrovac (see page 96).

Trogir (Formerly Traù)

Dalmatian Coast: Central Section

The small town of Trogir lies roughly in the middle of the Dalmatian Coast at the western end of the Kastelanski Riviera. The old town centre is built on an island in the channel running between the mainland and the island of Ciovo, and is linked to both shores by bridges. This compact little town is one of the best examples of a medieval town in the whole of Dalmatia. It is also one of the oldest settlements in the area.

In the third century BC the Greeks founded a colony here, which they called Tragurion on account of the many goats (*tragoi*) in the vicinity. Following the barbarian invasions it passed from Byzantine

Church, Trogir

Zadar

to Croat and then to Hungarian rule. From 1422 to 1797 it belonged
to Venice. It then passed to Austria, and remained so until 1918 apart
from a short period of French rule between 1806 and 1814. Since
1918 it has been part of Yugoslavia. It was a bishopric from 1026 until
1822.

   The visitor enters the city from the north via the so-called Land
Gate (Kopnena Vrata). The narrow streets lead quickly into the main
square, next to which is the town's most impressive building, the
cathedral of **Sveti Lovre** (St Laurence). It was begun in the
thirteenth century, but was not completed until the fifteenth. The bell
tower came even later, and was not finished until the end of the
sixteenth century; it is one of the finest examples of Venetian Gothic
in the whole of Yugoslavia. The west portal is particularly beautiful,
being covered with fine sculptures by the great master Radovan.

   The interior contains yet more masterpieces: a canopied altar by a local artist called Mavro; a thirteenth-century marble pulpit; and the fifteenth-century Gothic choir-stalls by another native sculptor called Budislavic. The vestry contains a carved wooden chest, also from the fifteenth century. The small chapel leading off the north aisle is dedicated to Sveti Ivan Orsini (St John of Trogir). It is thought to be the best example in Yugoslavia of Renaissance architecture, and is the creation of Niccolo Fiorentino and Andrija Alesi. The baptistry near the west door was also created by Alesi.

Immediately opposite the cathedral is the **Palaca Cipiko**, with its Venetian Gothic façade. The **town hall** is also next to the main square, and though originally built in the fifteenth century, it was largely rebuilt in the nineteenth. One particularly good feature is the outside staircase in the courtyard, which has been rebuilt in the form of the original fifteenth-century structure.

Also overlooking the square is an impressive fourteenth-century loggia, with six columns along the front; it was originally a place of execution. Next to it is a fifteenth-century clock tower that was once part of a church.

If one leaves the main square to the right of the town hall, one quickly comes to the thirteenth-century church of **Sveti Ivan** (St John). It contains some fine medieval frescos, and now houses a stone collection.

The street that leaves the main square past the loggia leads to the church of **Sveta Barbara**. This is the oldest church building in the town, dating from the ninth century. A short distance further along the same street is the **Benedictine convent**, which has a number of interesting features: the church of Sveti Nikola, and fine cloisters.

At the far end of the street is the so-called Sea Gate (Morska Vrata), which actually looks out across the channel to the island of Ciovo. The old city walls have been preserved on either side of it. To the left of the gate (leaving the town) is another small loggia that is now used for selling fish. The column standing on the harbour quay dates back to the early seventeenth century.

If one goes right along the quay, one soon sees the church of **Sveti Dominik** on the right. This fourteenth-century building contains some fine altars, a painting by the younger Palma, and the tomb of the Sobota family, carved by Niccolo Fiorentino in the Renaissance style.

The end of the quay is guarded by two massive fifteenth- century forts called the **Kastel Kamerlengo** and the **Kula Sveta Marka**. In between them is a small monument in the form of a roofless temple. It is dedicated to Marshal Marmont, and is a reminder of the short period of French rule.

A bridge crosses the channel to the island of Ciovo (see the Dalmatian Islands*), where the village of **Ciovo** is effectively a suburb of Trogir. Four kilometres to the east of the bridge is the Dominican monastery of **Sveti Kriz** (St Cross), which has a set of old choir-stalls and a small cloister.

The nearest bathing beaches are Saldun Bay on the west side of the island of Ciovo, and Seget on the mainland, 2km to the west of Trogir. Just outside and to the north of Trogir is the hotel village of Medena.

There are several places to visit on the mainland, the nearest being the **Kastelanski Riviera** or Bay of Seven Castles to the east. At the opposite end of the bay are Solin*, site of the Roman city of Salona, and the ancient port of Split*. Visitors are also recommended to make a short trip inland via Klis to the lovely little town of Sinj (see Split*).

Veglio *see* **Krk Island**

Zadar (Formerly Zara)

Dalmatian Coast: Northern Section

Zadar today has a population of 116,000, and was once the capital of Dalmatia. In spite of severe destruction wrought by Allied bombers during World War II, the town still retains much of its rich cultural heritage. The old town is concentrated on the north side of a long peninsula, which faces the mainland across the harbour. The modern suburbs stretch out along the coast both to the north and the south.

The city was originally founded by the Liburnians, and was called ladera by the Romans. It became a Roman colony under Emperor Augustus, after which it flourished as a port. It became a major city in the Byzantine Empire, and remained so even after the seventh century, when the Slavs occupied most of the coast. But it eventually fell to the kings of Croatia.

The city then became subject to repeated Venetian attacks in a war that was to continue for centuries. In 1202 it was taken by the Venetians, who almost razed it to the ground. There followed another period of Croatian rule, before the Venetians took firm possession in the fourteenth century. There were several Turkish attacks in later centuries, but it nonetheless remained under Venetian rule until 1797.

The Austrians ruled from then until World War I, apart from a short period of French rule between 1806 and 1814. The city came to Italy in 1920 under the Treaty of Rapallo. During World War II it was occupied by Germany and handed back to Italy together with the rest of the Dalmatian Coast. It finally came to Yugoslavia in 1944.

The old city still retains the grid pattern of streets that character-ised the original Roman colony. The main access is still via the old Land Gate (Porta Terra-Firma or Kopmena Vrata), which was built by Sanmicheli in the sixteenth century on the neck of land linking the old city with the mainland. One other old gate still remains — the so-called Sea Gate (Porta Marina or Morska Vrata). This was also built in the sixteenth century, and looks out across the harbour to the north.

The broad square just to the north of the Land Gate is called the Trg Oslobodjenja or Terasa Pet Bunara (Five Pumps Terrace). The five pumps are still there; they are no longer working, but they were once connected to a large water cistern. There are a few remains of the old city walls, including a thirteenth-century tower called the Bablija Kula. There is a Roman column in the middle of the square, and the remains of a Roman triumphal arch have been uncovered nearby.

To the north of the square is the church of **Sveti Simun** (St Simeon). It is not known when it was originally built, but much of the present structure dates from the seventeenth century. Its chief claim to fame is the silver shrine of St Simeon, which was given to the town by Queen Elisabeth of Hungary in 1308.

Further to the north-west is Zadar's main central square, the Narodni Trg or People's Square. There is a Renaissance loggia on the south side. Opposite are the town hall and the old police station

Sveti Donat, Zadar

— a late eighteenth-century Baroque building with a clock tower that is now the **Museum of Ethnography**.

If one continues along the main street, the Ulica Ive Ribara Lole, and takes the second street on the right towards the Sea Gate, one soon comes across a beautiful church on the right next to the Sarajevska Ulica. The church of **Sveti Krsevan** is a twelfth-century Romanesque structure with an impressive façade and an apse decorated with columns and sculptures.

If one carries straight on along the Ulica Ive Ribara Lole, one soon finds the cathedral of **Sveta Stosija** (St Anastasia) on the left. It was badly damaged by bombs, but has since been beautifully restored. The west front dates from 1324, and is the finest Romanesque façade in the whole of Dalmatia. The elaborate choir-stalls are from the fifteenth century, and the magnificent high altar is from the fourteenth. The cathedral contains a number of valuable treasures, with paintings including works by Carpaccio. The tower was begun in the fifteenth century, but was not finished until the end of the nineteenth. There is a marvellous view from the top.

The broad square to the south-west of the cathedral, the Trg Zeleni, is the site of the former Roman forum. It is strewn with numerous Roman remains uncovered by archaeologists. One Corinthian column is still intact, having been used as a pillory in the Middle Ages.

The adjacent church of **Sveti Donat** was built of stone from the buildings that had previously stood in the forum. This massive octagonal structure was founded in the ninth century by Bishop Donatus of Zara, and is one of the most outstanding examples of early Dalmatian architecture. For many centuries it was used as a warehouse and wine cellar, and until recently it was the headquarters of the Archaeological Museum. (The main museum building is now at the far end of the quay on the south side of the peninsula; it contains a vast collection of pre-Roman, Roman and medieval finds.)

The church of S**veti Marija** is to the south-east of the forum on the Ulica General Ante Bonina. It was badly damaged by bombs, but has since been restored. Several fine frescos were discovered in the course of the restoration work. The clock tower was built in the twelfth century.

There are two more churches to the north-west of the forum along the Ulica Petra Preradovica. **Sveti Ilija** has a fine collection of icons, while the thirteenth-century church of **Sveti Franjo** contains some impressive paintings, a set of fourteenth-century choir-stalls and a lovely eleventh-century crucifix.

The city of Zadar is a busy industrial port. Its best-known export is maraschino, a liqueur made from the stones and juice of a bitter-tasting cherry called the marasca that is grown in the surrounding region.

There is an open-air swimming pool in the modern part of the town. The nearest beach is at **Borik** out to the north-west, where there is a holiday village among the pinewoods next to a good sandy beach.

The harbour is a busy one, with regular ferry services to Ancona in Italy and to Preko on the nearby island of Ugljan. There are numerous other boat excursions available to others of the Dalmatian Islands*, and to various ports along the coast.

Visitors are recommended to make a short excursion to **Nin** (Nona), which lies 18km to the north along a small side-road. Though insignificant nowadays, it can still boast a long and illustrious history. It was called Aenona in Roman times, and was the capital of the province of Liburnia. There are several remnants of the forum and of a temple of Diana, and some tombs have also been unearthed there.

Nin was particularly important during the period of Croatian rule, when it was one of several seats of the Croatian kings. The ninth-century church of **Sveti Kriz** (St Cross) is a marvellous example of pre-medieval architecture. This small building was originally used for coronations. Nin is also well known as the seat of Bishop Grgur Ninski, who campaigned for the use of Croat as a liturgical language. The eleventh-century church of **Sveti Nikola** stands on a hill, and is visble for miles around. Several ancient Illyrian cemeteries have been found in the surrounding area.

Those who have not already been to Obrovac and Novigrad (see page 63) are recommended to visit them from Zadar, the round trip being little more than 100km. The route leaves Zadar via the airport and Donji Zemunik. After 24km the road arrives at **Smilcic**, where a number of Liburnian grave mounds and New Stone Age remains have been discovered in the vicinity.

There is a turning here for **Novigrad** (8km) next to the Novigradsko More (Novigrad Sea). The road from Novigrad to Karin (8km) first climbs steeply before descending to the shores of the Karinsko More (Karin Sea). On the hillside above the scattered village of **Karin** are the remains of the former Roman settlement of Corinium. Further along the shore is a small fifteenth-century Franciscan monastery.

The road then climbs over a small pass, with some iine views of the mountains and a certain amount of forest. Sixteen kilometres from Karin it arrives at the pretty little town of **Obrovac**. Obrovac is described on page 63, together with the direct return route to Zadar via Maslenica.

6 ADVICE TO TOURISTS

Travelling to Yugoslavia

Air Travel

For those who wish to plan their holidays independently, the airports along the coast are all well served by flights from the UK, the USA and Canada, and not only from the main international airports. The main destinations (apart from the international airports at Ljubljana, Zagreb and Belgrade) are Pula, Split and Dubrovnik, with further connections to Rijeka, Zadar and Tivat. Details are readily available from travel agents.

Boat Travel

Apart from the Channel and North Sea crossings for road or rail travellers starting in the UK, there are many interesting possibilities for those wishing to visit Yugoslavia by boat.

There are passenger routes from Rijeka to all the main islands, ports and resorts along the coast, with similar services from Venice and Trieste in Italy. The journey time from Rijeka to Dubrovnik is about 24 hours, from Venice to Dubrovnik between 30 and 40 hours. Cars can be carried on some of these services.

The car ferries from the Italian Adriatic ports make it possible to plan a combined Italian and Yugoslavian holiday. The main routes are Ancona to Zadar or Dubrovnik, Pescara to Split, and Bari to Dubrovnik. Most services operate only during the summer, when early booking is essential. Details are available from travel agents and automobile associations.

Also worth mentioning here are the various cruises available, whether of the Adriatic only or as part of a longer Mediterranean cruise. Visits to the ports are usually combined with various excursions to local places of interest. This is undoubtedly one of the most interesting and relaxing ways of visiting the coast of Yugoslavia.

Car Travel

A car provides the most independent means of visiting the coast of Yugoslavia. A route from the United Kingdom will vary depending on the starting point and destination, but is likely to go through Belgium or France, Germany or Switzerland, Austria or Italy. If time allows, it is worth taking a different route either way. Car travellers with less time may care to circumvent the long journey through Europe by taking advantage of autorail (see below) or car hire services (see page 201).

Coach Travel

Apart from coach holidays organised by various package companies, there are international coach routes with connections to Yugoslavian resorts. Details can be obtained from travel agents.

Package Holidays

This is by far the simplest and most comfortable way of visiting Yugoslavia, as all the organisation is done for you. There are countless different possibilities, offering travel by plane or ship combined with coach or rail. Hotel bookings are included, together with optional excursions if required.

Public Transport Prices

Fares are generally relatively low in Yugoslavia, whatever the mode of transport. This applies equally to railways, buses, boats and even taxis.

Rail Travel

The Yugoslavian coast is well served by international trains, with carriages travelling direct from several cross-Channel and European ports. The journey is a long one, so it is worth the extra cost of reserving a reclining seat or a bed in a sleeping compartment if one is travelling overnight. During the high season it is essential to book well in advance.

Visitors with cars may wish to take advantage of the international autorail services, which again offer sleeping accommodation. They only run on certain days in the week, so pre-booking is essential, especially in the high season.

Travel Within Yugoslavia

Information
Plenty of information is available from local tourist offices and travel agents, who also make bookings and reservations.

Boat Travel
The main shipping routes along the coast have already been mentioned on page 198. These same routes can also be used for much shorter journeys. In addition there are a large number of local services between ports along the coast or between the islands and the mainland.

Hydrofoil services have so far been introduced in Porec, Pula, Opatija, Rijeka, Split and Dubrovnik. Some are incorporated within the main transport network, while others are used for special excursions. In summer, hydrofoils also run services to certain towns on the Italian coast.

There are numerous ferries linking the islands with the mainland. The majority carry only foot passengers, but cars can be taken on the following routes:

Brestova to Porozina (Cres Island)
Rijeka to Porozina (Cres Island)
Crikvenica to Silo (Cres Island)
Senj to Baska (Krk Island) (pre-booking necessary)
Baska (Krk Island) to Lopar (Rab Island) (pre-booking
    necessary)
Senj to Lopar (Rab Island)
Jablanac to Pudarica (Rab Island)
Pudarica (Rab Island) to Stara Novalja (Pag Island) (on
    request)
Jablanac to Stara Novalja (Pag Island)
Karlobag to Pag (Pag Island)
Zadar to Preko (Ugljan Island)

Biograd to Tkon (Pasman Island)
Split to Rogac (Solta Island)
Split to Vela Luka (Korcula Island)
Split to Vira (Hvar Island)
Split to Starigrad (Hvar Island)
Split to Supetar (Brac Island)
Makarska to Sumartin (Brac Island)
Drvenik to Sucuraj (Hvar Island)
Drvenik to Trpanj (Peljesac Peninsula)
Kardeljevo to Trpanj (Peljesac Peninsula)
Orebic (Peljesac Peninsula) to Korcula (Korcula Island)
Kamenari to Lepetane (Gulf of Kotor)

Bus Travel
The bus has become the chief mode of transport within Yugoslavia.
The many bus companies run regular services along the coast,
together with a few into the hinterland and several on the larger
islands. All of them are available to tourists, though being primarily
for local use they are often very busy.

Car Hire Services
All the towns and major resorts offer car hire services, both with and
without chauffeurs. The firms function both locally and internationally. Autotehna, for example, is the local representative for Avis,
while Kompas fulfils the interests of Hertz. It is even possible to hire
a car 'one-way' between two European countries. One might, for
example, fly out to Dubrovnik, hire a car as far as Venice and fly back
from there.

Maps
A good map is essential for driving in Yugoslavia. The best policy is
to buy a general map of the whole coast, plus more detailed maps of
the areas of specific interest. Suitable maps can generally be bought
or ordered at local booksellers here.

Motoring in Yugoslavia

All the main roads in northern Yugoslavia have good tarmac surfaces. The same applies to the so-called Jadranska magistrala or

Adriatic Highway that serves the whole coast from Ankaran in the north to Ulcinj in the south. It has no steep climbs, and plenty of lay-bys and viewing points.

The roads in the interior still have a lot of work to be done on them. The route through Karlovac and the Plitvice Lakes is fortunately quite decent. The same applies to most of the road going north from Metkovic via Mostar to Sarajevo; it has a branch going via Jajce and Banja Luka to connect with the main motorway from Ljubljana to Skopje.

On other routes, one must always make allowances for possible sections of unmade road, which can only be avoided by long detours. But these once notorious roads no longer pose the problems that they used to, provided that one drives with the caution appropriate to the road conditions.

Even the main coast road cannot always be driven very fast. Though in decent condition, it is very twisty in places, and is subject to obstacles and even blockages where landslides occur. One should also bear in mind that local drivers do not always pay much attention to the rules of the road. Horses and donkeys are still a very popular mode of transport.

In the autumn and spring, the bora can sometimes pose a danger to traffic along the coast. It has been known to blow so suddenly and with such force as to cause traffic accidents and even fatalities. On such days it is better to wait for the wind to die down before continuing one's journey.

Emergency Services

These are run by the Yugoslav motoring association, the AMSJ or Auto-moto savez Jugoslavije. Its vehicles patrol all major roads from 8am to 8pm every day. They can be recognised from the club badge and from the following message in large letters: — POMOC-INFOR-MACIJE

One can telephone the AMSJ for help or information by dialling **987**. Assistance can also be given from local AMSJ offices. Their services are free to members of equivalent national motoring associations or of the international organisations AIT and FTA. But payment is required for spares, motor fuel and oil, and also for towing. The headquarters address is AMSJ, Ruzveltova 18, 11000 Beograd.

Motor Fuel

Motorists should always use high-octane fuel in Yugoslavia. Filling stations are to be found in sufficient numbers, but it is nonetheless advisable to fill up often, and always to fill the tank full. Note also that a large number of filling stations are closed at lunch time.

Motor Fuel Prices

No up-to-date figures can be given for these in view of the current variation in world oil prices. Motor fuel coupons are available at border posts, which can entail a saving of up to 10 per cent on the price of fuel. In March 1986 there were about fifty filling stations in the whole of Yugoslavia where lead-free motor fuel was available.

Motor Spares

Given the often rough surfaces, it is worth taking a good selection of spares. The tyres should be in good condition, and the spare should be equally good. Drivers are recommended to take a suitable tool box with spares such as a fanbelt, spark plugs, fuses, spare bulbs and contact set. These are essential for any long journey abroad, and especially in a country such as Yugoslavia where garages are not very common. There are garages in the main towns, however, and Yugoslav mechanics are generally quite good at improvising when the need arises.

Traffic Regulations

These are mostly the same as in other European countries. Traffic signs also correspond closely to the international code, and even when different they are not difficult to understand. The roads are generally well signposted, though the signposts are often less obvious than one could wish for.

Normal speed limits are as follows: 60km/h (36mph) in built-up areas; 120km/h (72mph) on motorways; 100km/h (60mph) on main roads; 80km/h (48mph) on side-roads. Any other restrictions are clearly indicated by signs. Cars towing caravans or trailers must stay below 80km/h (48mph). Tolls are charged on motorways and on some main roads.

Hooting is prohibited at any time in big cities such as Ljubljana, Zagreb and Belgrade, and is prohibited everywhere else at night between 10pm and 5am. A first-aid kit and a warning triangle are strongly recommended. Two warning triangles are needed for vehicles with caravans or trailers. There are laws against drinking and driving. Children less than 12 years of age and intoxicated persons are not allowed on the front seat. Safety belts must always be worn, and all accidents must be reported to the police. The police telephone number is **94**, or **92** in cases of emergency.

Tips for Travellers

Car Travel Documents

An ordinary British or American driving licence is sufficient for visitors to Yugoslavia. The international Green Card is not compulsory, but is strongly advised for insurance purposes. Visitors without a Green Card are required to take out a short-term third-party insurance policy at the border. Any driver who does not own the car must have an authorisation from the owner that has been endorsed by the insurance authorities or an automobile association. Every vehicle must carry the national identification code.

A special customs declaration is required for caravans or trailers, and for spare cans of motor fuel. Caravan owners are advised to make an inventory of the contents of their caravan, and to have this endorsed by customs on entry into Yugoslavia; this will simplify matters when leaving the country. Visitors staying longer than 3 months must fill in a special customs declaration form. If for any reason the car has to be left behind in Yugoslavia, then the driver must report this to the local customs authorities.

Motor fuel coupons are available from some banks and travel agents, and in particular from automobile clubs and at border posts. They are valid for 3 months from the date of issue, and can entail a saving of about 10 per cent on the price of motor fuel.

Clothing

Light clothing is not easy to forget when visiting Yugoslavia in the summer. But one should also remember to take at least one warm pullover for cool evenings, sea trips or visiting caves. A light raincoat is also advisable.

Currency and Prices

The Yugoslav unit of currency is the dinar, which consists of 100 paras. There are coins worth 5, 10, 20 and 50 paras, and 1, 2, 5, 10, 20, 50 and 100 dinars; banknotes are worth 10, 20, 50, 100, 500, 1,000 and 5,000 dinars.

The exchange rate varies enormously from day to day, and also depends on the denomination of the notes being exchanged. Travellers are advised to enquire at their local bank regarding the current exchange rate.

Customs and Currency Regulations

There is no duty on personal luggage and belongings that are brought into Yugoslavia. This can include the following items: personal jewellery; food for the journey; 2 cameras with five films; a small cine camera with 2 films; 1 pair of binoculars; 1 pocket calculator; 1 portable musical instrument; 1 portable record player with 10 records; 1 portable radio; 1 portable television; 1 portable typewriter; 1 racing boat; camping equipment; a bicycle; sports equipment; inexpensive motor spares. The following quantities of other goods may also be imported without paying duty: 200 cigarettes or 50 cigars or 250g tobacco or a total of 250g of all the above products; 1 litre of wine; $1/_4$ litre of spirits; $1/_4$ litre of eau de cologne and a small amount of perfume.

There are no limits on the amount of foreign currency that may be taken in or out of Yugoslavia. There are, however, limits on the movement of Yugoslav currency, of which only 10,000 dinars in 1,000-dinar notes may be taken in or out at the first entrance or exit. If any consecutive visits are made in the same year, the amount of dinars that can be carried into or out of Yugoslavia is limited to 5,000 dinars. Currency may only be exchanged at banks, *bureaux de change*, hotels and specially licensed travel and tourist offices. Eurocheques are accepted by Yugoslav banks. Receipts should be retained for all transactions, as questions may be asked on leaving the country.

Electrical Points

220V alternating current is general throughout Yugoslavia.

Health and Insurance

Visitors should enquire at their local health and social security offices about mutual health arrangements and procedures in case of accident or illness abroad. At all events, it is essential to insure against such eventualities. Medical insurance is normally included in holiday insurance policies, which may be arranged in conjunction with travel bookings.

Visitors should always take sufficient quantities of any medication they are likely to need, bearing in mind the climate. Luggage should always be kept to a minimum, and should be included in holiday insurance arrangements.

National Holidays

1 and 2 January (everywhere)
1 and 2 May (everywhere)
4 July (everywhere)
7 July (only in Serbia)
13 July (only in Montenegro)
22 July (only in Slovenia)
27 July (only in Bosnia–Hercegovina and Croatia)
2 August (only in Macedonia)
11 October (only in Macedonia)
1 November (only in Slovenia)
29 and 30 November (everywhere)

Opening Hours

There are no standard opening hours, and opening hours generally are subject to continual change. Banks are generally open from 8am to 11am, offices from 8am to 2pm. Travel agents and *bureaux de change* are open from 8am to 12 noon and from 4pm to 7pm. On Saturdays they are only open in the morning, while banks and offices are closed all day. In towns and major tourist centres some offices stay open through the afternoon or even all day.

Shops are normally open from 8am to 12 noon and from 4pm to 8pm (or 7pm in the north of the country). Big shops and department stores often stay open throughout the afternoon. On Saturdays most shops close at 1pm or 2pm, and Sunday is a public holiday. Shops in tourist areas often ignore the normal opening hours, preferring to open at times convenient to their customers.

Passport Requirements

A passport without a visa is sufficient for visitors from the United Kingdom staying in the country for not more than 3 months. A visa is required for a longer stay. American and Canadian visitors are advised to contact their consulate for information regarding application for a visa.

Souvenirs

Yugoslavia now manufactures most of its souvenirs to satisfy the enormous demand from tourists. But handmade goods are still available from some souvenir shops, and especially from market stalls. Goods on offer include beautiful lace and embroidery, carved figures, leather goods (including traditional footwear), carpets and wall-hangings, ceramics and filigree work.

A Turkish coffee mill makes an ideal souvenir, together with a Turkish coffee service. Another possibility is a set of glasses or beakers with Slavic or oriental designs. Local drinks such as slivovitz or maraschino are also very good value.

Some shops in tourist areas offer a 10 per cent reduction on goods bought in exchange for foreign currency or travellers' cheques.

Tipping

Hotel and restaurant prices are inclusive of service charges, but a small tip is usually expected in addition. This should normally be about 10 per cent with smaller bills, somewhat less with larger bills. Taxi drivers, luggage porters and hairdressers also expect their prices to be rounded up accordingly, and a driver usually tips a filling station attendant.

Accommodation

The coast of Yugoslavia offers a wide choice of different types of holiday accommodation, including hotels, guesthouses, motels, villas, holiday camps and private rooms. It is more difficult to find accommodation in places further inland, simply because they are less geared towards the tourist industry.

Visitors wishing to book a private room in a particular town or resort should write to the local tourist office, addressing their letter to the *Turisticki drustvo* or *Turisticki biro* in the place concerned. One can usually count on English being spoken at the larger tourist offices or travel agents, or those accustomed to English-speaking tourists. In other places there can be communication problems. Addresses and telephone numbers of many tourist information offices may be found on page 229

Where to Stay and Places to Visit

The most popular bathing resorts are Portoroz, Lovran, Opatija, Crikvenica, Rab, Makarska, Hvar and Dubrovnik. Two other favourite tourist haunts are Tucepi and the beach at Brela. The Montenegrin coastal resorts of Hercegnovi, Sveti Stefan and Budva provide excellent hotel accommodation, while the Istrian resorts of Umag, Porec and Rovinj are similarly ideal for bathing.

Besides this, there are numerous more recently built hotel developments next to pleasant bathing beaches; these include Pula-Podstinje, Medulin, Rabac, Zadar, Biograd, the Kastelanski Riviera near Split, and Podgora. Other resorts in pleasant surroundings include Moscenicka Draga, Novi Vinodolski, Mlini and Cavtat, plus a whole host of smaller and rather quieter resorts, both on the islands and in the area around Zadar and Sibenik.

Those interested in art and architecture should visit historic centres such as Pula, Rijeka, Zadar, Sibenik, Split and Dubrovnik. These are of interest not only for their own sake, but for the things to see in the surrounding towns and villages.

The choice is much greater for those interested in the beauties of nature, for the whole coast has more than its fair share of beautiful scenery. Wherever one decides to stay, there will be plenty of lovely places to go.

Guesthouse Accommodation

Another option available is to rent a room in a private house. This is normally organised by hotels or tourist agencies, who allocate the rooms and handle the payment of bills. Sometimes, however, individual landlords offer their services directly to tourists at the point of arrival, either at the bus stop or on the pier.

Private guesthouse accommodation can be rather basic, but is normally very clean. There are exceptions to this, and one can occasionally be treated to an amazing level of luxury and comfort. But it is unusual to find a wash basin in one's own room, and one normally has only the shared use of a bathroom.

Guesthouses are classified in five categories according to location and standard of accommodation. **L** signifies luxury standards, while categories **A** to **D** cover the more usual levels of service, none of which quite match up to hotels. Category **A**, for example, means that there is a bathroom and WC for every one or at most two double rooms; **B** is by far the most common category available.

There is normally a choice between full-board, half-board and bed-and-breakfast accommodation, but this must usually be stipulated in advance. There are price reductions available for longer stays — occasionally after only 3 days, but sometimes only after a fortnight. There is also a vast difference in prices between high season, mid-season and low season.

Hotel and Villa Accommodation

Modern hotels are equipped to the usual international standard, and most rooms have a WC and bath or shower. Many of the older buildings have been renovated and re-equipped to modern standards. The increased demand during the high season means that catering services are often overloaded, and personal service is sometimes adversely affected in some of the larger hotel complexes and holiday villages.

Large colonies of holiday villas have sprung up along the coast to satisfy the increased demand from tourists. Some villas and flats are hired out as self-contained units, with all facilities laid on for a self-catering holiday.

Often, however, villas are grouped around a large central building providing restaurant and other facilities. Such accommodation is usually made up of double rooms, each equipped with shower and WC. Full board is normally the only option available in complexes such as these.

The vast increase in demand has caused a massive building boom, with gigantic hotel pavilions accommodating as many as

2,000 or 3,000 beds. The restaurants are correspondingly vast, and there is a wide choice of sport and leisure activities available.

Most of the major tourist centres have motels, which offer the usual international standard of service and accommodation.

Hotel prices are categorised according to the standard of service and comfort provided. Guesthouse prices vary similarly, so that the highest prices are more than twice the lowest during the high season. Considerable reductions are given in the mid-season and low season. A local tax is charged in addition.

Prices also vary enormously depending on the locality. Hotel prices are much higher, for example, in the cities and in the larger or more popular resorts such as Opatija, Dubrovnik and places around Makarska and towards the southern end of the coast.

Camping

Yugoslavia offers a wide range of pleasantly laid-out camping sites for visitors with tents or caravans. They are often outside the main tourist areas, and provide peace and quiet in addition to the beautiful scenery.

Visitors who wish to set up camp outside the officially designated sites must obtain a permit from the tourist office (*turisticki biro*) or local authorities. Camping wild is not advisable, as hefty fines are imposed for any damage to the environment.

Information

The Turisticki Savez Jugoslavije and the Savezna Privredna Komora both produce the following items each year:

- a price list of hotel and villa accommodation;
- a guide to the so-called Jugohotels — a countrywide federation of some 200 hotels of higher-than-average standard;
- a full list of camping sites available.

These lists are available from travel agents or from the Yugoslav National Tourist Office.

Food and Drink

Only in towns and tourist areas can one rely on finding a wide range of eating places. In some places the only food available is in hotel dining rooms. Larger towns, on the other hand, provide a much better choice, ranging from snack bars and self-service restaurants to the more select establishments, where local delicacies are served. The *slasticarna* is like a cake shop cum coffee bar, where guests are offered a choice of cakes, pastries and ices. The *gostiona* is a private restaurant, where visitors may sample local specialities.

Hotel cuisine tends not to be very imaginative. At breakfast, for example, instant coffee is often the norm, as elsewhere around the Mediterranean. The scope is somewhat better in larger establishments, where guests may either eat *à la carte* or else choose between different set menus.

Restaurants on the coast offer a combination of Viennese, international and local cuisine. Unusually for coastal regions, meat dishes tend to be better prepared than fish ones. The food may be oilier and more highly spiced than one is perhaps accustomed to at home, but it is nonetheless easily digestible. The soups and salads are particularly good; the desserts on offer include gâteaux, strudels, ices and fruit. There is also a fascinating variety of goat's cheeses to choose from.

A Menu Guide
Menus are often given in several languages, including English. But it is still useful to be able to decipher a standard menu in Serbo-Croat. The following guide may be of help:

Soups (*juha, čorba*)
bujon — *bouillon*, broth
juha od paradajza — tomato soup
juha sa krompirom — potato soup
juha so rezancima — noodle soup

Meat (*meso*)
bečki šnicl obložen — Vienna schnitzel
bravetina, ovčetina — mutton

govedina — beef
janjetina — lamb
naravni šnicl — veal cutlet
pečenje, pržolica — joint, roast
šunka — ham
svenjetina — pork
teletina — veal

Game (*divljač*)
jelen — venison (of red deer)
srnetina — venison (of roe deer)
zec — hare

Poultry (*perad, živina*)
guska — goose
piletina — chicken
plovka — duck

Fish (riba)
bakalar — cod
haringa — herring
jegulja —eel
pastrva — trout
skuša — mackerel
štuka — pike
tunjevina — tuna

Vegetables (*povrće*)
cvjetača, karfiol — Brussels sprouts
gjive, pečurke — mushrooms
grašak — peas
kelj, kupus, — cabbage
krastavac — cucumber
krumpiri — potatoes
leća —lentils
mrkva — carrots
paradajz, rajčica — tomato
pasulj — beans
salata — salad, lettuce
špinat — spinach

rezanci — noodles
pirinač, riža — rice
šećer — sugar
so — salt
biber — pepper
gorušica — mustard
ocat — vinegar
ulje —oil
jaje — egg
rovito — soft-boiled (egg)
tvrdo kuvano — hard-boiled (egg)
jaja pržena — fried eggs
omlet — omelette

hljeb, kruh — bread
prepek — toast
zemička — roll
kolači —cakes
torta — tart, flan
sladoled — ice cream

Fruit (*voće*)
breskva — peach
dinja, lubenica — melon
grepfrut — grapefruit
grožđje — grape
jabuka — apple
kruška —pear
limun — lemon
naranča — orange
šljiva — plum
tresňja — cherry

Local Specialities
bakalar — cod
baklava — a sweet made of honey, walnuts and almonds
brodet — sea fish prepared with paprika
burek — pasties with various fillings
ćevapčići — spiced, minced, grilled meat

cŏrba — sour soup

čulbastija — grilled steak with raw onions

djuveč — meat (or occasionally fish) risotto, made with rice, tomatoes, red peppers, onions, and sometimes with carrots and potatoes

hajduškićevap — various roast meats

kalamar — squid

kapama — lamb with onions, spinach and soured cream or other vegetables

lonac bosanski — Bosnian stew, made with various meats and vegetables

mučkalica — meat with onions, chillies and pepper

musaka — a baked dish of minced pork or beef with eggs and vegetables, including pieces of pumpkin or marrow

pilav — rice with meat and spices

plavi patlidžani — stuffed aubergines

punjeni pljeskavića — grilled rissoles with onions

pršut — air-dried ham

punjena paprika — red peppers stuffed with rice and mince in a tomato sauce

ražnjici — pork or veal kebab

riblja cŏrba — fish soup

ricet — stewed beans and pot-barley

riza sa graškom — rice with peas

sarma — stuffed vegetables, especially cabbage or vine leaves

sataraž — steamed tomatoes, red peppers and onions with egg or slices of sausage

Drinks

Wine is the favourite drink in Yugoslavia, where even the simplest country wines can taste good. Yugoslav beer (*pivo*) is also very popular. Tap water should be avoided, but mineral water provides a cheap and plentiful substitute. Lemonade and other fizzy drinks are also very reasonable in price. The various fruit juices are very good, including fresh lemon and raspberry juices. Another very thirst-quenching drink is spričer (spritzer) — a sparkling mixture of one part wine to two parts mineral water.

Self-catering
In the towns there are plentiful provisions to supply individual needs. The choice is more limited in small village shops, where one can also run into communication problems. But in the towns there are usually plenty of self-service shops.

Spirits
Of the spirits on offer in Yugoslavia, *šljivovica* (slivovitz) is undoubtedly the best; it is a kind of plum brandy. The most popular liqueur is *maročkin* (maraschino), made from marasca cherries, especially in the area around Zadar. The various bitters include *vlahovac* and *istra bitter*, a kind of campari.

Tobacco Goods
In Yugoslavia tobacco goods are available at tobacconists', general stores and also at restaurants. There are many different brands of cigarettes, but all of them are made out of tobacco from Macedonia or Hercegovina. The tobaccos are light, and are usually of the Turkish or Greek kind. The best-known brands are Arena, Drina, Hercegovina, Jadran, Morava, Mostar and Prilep. Filter cigarettes are also available. Yugoslavian cigars tend to be less popular with visitors from abroad.

Turkish Coffee
Excellent Turkish coffee is available throughout Yugoslavia at very reasonable prices. It is made and served in the traditional fashion in a little brass jug. Nothing is added, although the coffee already contains a little sugar.

Wines
Yugoslavia has fewer specific types of wine than countries such as Germany and France. The best white wines include *vugava*, *slovenski rizling*, *posip*, *zilavka* and *grk*. The best red wines to try are *dingač*, *opolo*, *plavac*, *refoška*, *vipava* and *malvazija*. *Omiš* is a kind of muscatel, while *bakarska vodica* is a popular sparkling wine, and *prošek* is an excellent sweet wine.

Sport and Leisure Activities

Angling
There are plenty of opportunities for fishing in Yugoslavia. However, those wishing to fish in lakes or rivers must first obtain a permit from the local authorities in exchange for the appropriate fee. Sea fishing, on the other hand, is free.

Diving and Snorkelling
The clear waters of the Mediterranean are ideal for such activities. However, a permit must be obtained from the local authorities for the use of diving equipment and underwater cameras. A permit is similarly required for underwater fishing. Those interested should write to the following address for details both of the regulations and of the facilities available: Savez za sportski ribolov na moru i podvone aktivnosti SFRJ, Matije Gupca 2, Rijeka.

Evening Entertainment
The larger resorts lay on a wide variety of evening activities, including music and dancing. The same is true of many of the larger hotels and restaurants. Bars and nightclubs are also to be found in some of the more exclusive holiday resorts. Casinos have so far been established at Dubrovnik, Opatija, Portoroz, Pula, Umag and Sveti Stefan.

Hunting
Hunting is a major sport in Yugoslavia, where game is particularly abundant. A special hunting permit must first, however, be obtained from the hunting association of the appropriate constituent republic. Further details about acquiring a permit can be obtained from the Yugoslav Hunting Association, whose address is as follows: Savez lovackih organizacija Jugoslavije, Alekse Nenadovica 23, Beograd. The Yugoslav National Tourist Office will also offer assistance in obtaining a permit.

Nudist and Naturist Beaches
The Yugoslavian authorities make ample provision for nude bathing and sunbathing. There is a substantial number of officially designated nudist beaches, all of which are clearly indicated as such. It is

not, however, advisable to bathe nude on beaches that have not been so designated.

Swimming and Bathing
The bays and coves that pepper the coast of Yugoslavia are a paradise for swimmers and bathers. But one should not count on finding sand, which is a rather rare commodity, especially on the Dalmatian Coast. The beaches are more commonly lined with rocks, stones or pebbles, though many of them have been adapted for bathing. Sometimes sand has been brought in from elsewhere, while on other occasions the shore has been overlaid with stone slabs or concrete. But at all events sandals or bathing shoes are advisable.

Walking and Rambling
There are plenty of opportunities for walks and rambles, and many of the more mountainous areas are well suited to hill-walking. Ramblers should not forget to take stout footwear for the purpose, as some of the paths are very rough.

Hill-walkers should note that there are a number of mountain huts among the various coastal mountain ranges. These are nearly all open during the summer, but no food or refreshments are provided. Hill-walking is a popular pastime with native Yugoslavs, and the best-known huts are well signposted. Details can be obtained from the various mountaineering organisations or from the Yugoslav National Tourist Office.

Other Facilities
Rowing and sailing boats, and sometimes motorboats as well, are available for hire at most ports and larger resorts. Facilities for water skiing are only provided at the major holiday centres. Other activities catered for include tennis, minigolf, archery, shooting, bowling, riding and cycling.

The Language

The ethnic variety of Yugoslavia is reflected in the variety of languages spoken. Fortunately, the three main languages are fairly closely related; they belong to the Southern Slav group of languages.

By far the majority of Yugoslavs speak Serbo-Croat, this being the main language of the constituent republics of Serbia, Croatia, Bosnia–Hercegovina and Montenegro. There are two stylistic varieties of Serbo-Croat, reflecting the religious allegiances of the speakers. The main difference between them is in the alphabet used. The mainly Catholic Croats of Croatia and Dalmatia use the Roman alphabet, while the mostly Orthodox Serbs of Serbia and Montenegro use the Cyrillic alphabet. They will also tend to call their language *hrvatski* (Croat) or *srpski* (Serb), depending on which alphabet they use. But there is otherwise little difference between the two.

The other two main languages, Slovene and Macedonian, are spoken in their respective constituent republics. The Slovenes, being mostly Catholic, write their language in Roman characters, while the mainly Orthodox Macedonians use Cyrillic characters. Macedonian is in many ways closer to Bulgarian than to Serbo- Croat. There are several non-Slavic minorities, each of which has its own language. These include Albanian (in Kosovo), Hungarian (in Vojvodina) and Turkish, with small pockets of German in the north and Italian on the coast.

Serbo-Croat is the mother tongue for the vast majority of the people that live on the coast, and is the first foreign language among the few who speak Slovene, Italian or Albanian. German and Italian are also commonly understood — French and English somewhat less so. Serbo-Croat is difficult grammatically, but is easier to pronounce than many other Eastern European languages. It also has the advantage of being phonetic (spoken as it is written). Visitors may therefore find it useful to take a Serbo-Croat phrasebook for help in communication. Although the characters č, ž and š have not been reproduced in the main body of this book, a short pronunciation guide is given below which will help with the reading of menus, street signs etc. The section on food and drink includes a large number of words and phrases commonly found on menus.

The Roman alphabet is used in most of the places covered in this guide. Visitors will only come across Cyrillic in Montenegro in the south and on trips into the interior. Also, the use of Roman script is on the increase in areas frequented by tourists, where traffic and road signs are often given in both forms.

The Pronunciation of Serbo-Croat

The five vowels are fairly simple, and are pronounced approximately as in the English words father, bed, machine, not and rule. The following consonants are similar to the English: **b, f, g, k, m, p, t, v**; the same applies to **d, l** and **n** unless they are followed by **j** (see below).

The **h** is like the **ch** in the Scottish lo**ch**, while the **j** is like the **y** in **y**es. One Serbo-Croat speciality is the **r**, which is rolled with the tongue; it is often treated as a vowel, as in the name of the island of Krk. The letters **q, w, x** and **y** are not used in Serbo-Croat. The following more complex consonants are explained in more detail:

c = ts as in ca**ts**

č = ch as in mu**ch**

ć = t and y run together, rather like the t in tune (British pronunciation)

dž = j as in **j**am

dj = d and y run together, rather like the (British) **d** in **d**une (often written as a d with a stroke thus: đ)

lj = l and y run together, rather like the (British) **l** in **l**ure (closer to the Italian **gli** or the Spanish **ll**)

nj = n and y run together, rather like the (British) n in **n**ew (closer to the French or Italian **gn** or the Spanish **ñ**)

s = hard s as in **s**at

ś = sh as in **sh**y

z = z as in **z**oo

ž = the soft sound of s in mea**s**ure

FURTHER INFORMATION

Places of Interest to Visit

Muzeji Cetinje
(Museums in Cetinje)
Titov trg b.b.
81250 Cetinje
☎ 086/21–265
Open: in season from 9am–7pm.

Creski muzej (Museum in Cres)
Palaca Arsan
51557 Cres
☎ 051/871–581
Open: in season from 9am–11pm
and from 3–5pm, closed on
Monday.

Dubrovacki muzej (Doge's
Palace)
Knezev dvor
50000 Dubrovnik
☎ 050/26–469, 28–469
Open: every day from 9am–1pm
and from 2pm–6.30pm.

Riznica katedrale (Museum in
Cathedral)
Marina Drzica 3
50000 Dubrovnik
☎ 26–445, 28–253
Open: in season from 9am–6pm.

**Muzej Dominikanskog
samostana** (Dominican
Monastery)
Izmedju vrata od Ploca 4
50000 Dubrovnik
☎ 050/26–472
Open: every day from 9am-12noon
and from 1–6pm.

Srpska pravoslavna crkva
(Serbian Orthodox Church)
Od puca 8
50000 Dubrovnik
☎ 050/26–260, 34–852
Open: every day from
10am–12noon.

**Muzej franjevackog
samostana** (Franciscan
Monastery)
Placa 2
50000 Dubrovnik
☎ 050/26–345
Open: every day from 8am–12noon
and from 2–4pm.

Katedrala u Hvaru (Cathedral in
Hvar)
58450 Hvar
☎ 058/74–152
Open: every day from 8am–7pm if
there are interested visitors.

Kapucinski samostan
(Capuchin Monastery)
Dokozica 1
51288 Karlobag
☎ 051/894–039
Open: in season every day from
9am-12noon and from 4–7pm.

Pokrajinski muzej (Museum in
Koper)
Kidriceva 19
66000 Koper
☎ 066/21–364
Open: every day in season from
9am–1pm and from 5–7pm.

Muzej Korcule (Museum in
Korcula)
Strossmayerov trg
50260 Korcula
☎ 711–420
Open: from 10am–12noon and
from 4–6pm, closed on Sunday.

Pomorski muzej Crne Gore
(Naval Museum)
Trg Bokeljske mornarice
85330 Kotor
☎ 082/25–146
Open: in season from 7am–8pm.

Malakoloski muzej
Zrtava fasizma 1
58300 Makarska
☎ 058/611–256
Open: in season from 9am–12pm
and from 5–8pm.

Moderna galerija (Modern
Gallery)
Dolac 1
51000 Rijeka
☎ 051/34–280
Open: every day from 10am–1pm
and from 5–8pm, closed on
Monday.

**Pomorski i istorijski muzej
hrvatskog primorja** (Naval and
History Museum)
Zrtava fasizma 18
51000 Rijeka
☎ 051/37–612

Prirodnjacki muzej (Natural
History Museum)
Setaliste Vladimira Nazora 3
51000 Rijeka
☎ 051/34–988
Open: from 9am–1pm and from
4–7pm in season.

Arheoloski muzej Istre
(Archaeological Museum)
Mate Balote 3
52000 Pula
☎ 052/33–024, 33–488
Open: every day from 9am–7pm.

**Zemaljski muzej Bosne i
Hercegovine** (Provincial
Museum)
Vojvode Putnika 7
71000 Sarajevo
☎ 071/35–322, 35–323
Open: from 9am–5pm.
On Saturday and Sunday from
9am–1pm.

Muzej grada Sarajeva (City
Museum)
Svetozara Markovica 54
71000 Sarajevo
☎ 071/535–586
Open: from 9am–5pm, closed on
Sunday.

**Muzej stare pravoslavne
crkve** (Serbian Orthodox Church)
Marsala Tita 87
71000 Sarajevo
☎ 071/538–286, 536–907
Open: from 6am–6pm, on Sunday
from 6–11am.

Muzej hrvatskih arheoloskih spomenika (Museum of Croatian Archaeological Monuments)
Ognjena Price b.b.
58000 Split
☎ 058/43–983, 45–255
Open: in season from 9am–1pm and from 6–8pm, on Sunday from 10am–12noon, closed on Monday.

Arheoloski muzej (Archaeological Museum)
Zrinsko-Frankopanska 25
58000 Split
☎ 058/44–574
Open: from 9am–1pm, on Sunday from 10am–12noon, closed on Monday.

Galerija Mestrovic (Mestrovic Gallery)
Setaliste Mose Pijade 46
58000 Split
☎ 058/42–483
Open: every day from 9am–6pm.

Riznica Splitske katedrale (Museum in Cathedral in Split)
Kraj Svetog Duje 5
58000 Split
☎ 058/42–589
Open: in season every day from 9am–6pm.

Etnografski muzej (Ethnographic Museum)
Iza loze 1
58000 Split
☎ 058/44–164
Open: in season from 9am–1pm and from 6–8pm, on Thursday from 9am–4pm.

Muzej grada Trogira (Museum of Trogir)
Gradska vrata 4
58220 Trogir
☎ 058/73–406
Open: in season from 9am–12noon and from 6–9pm.

Riznica Trogirske katedrale (Museum in Cathedral)
Narodni trg 2
58220 Trogir
☎ 058/73–426
Open: in season from 9am–12noon and from 3–7pm.

Arheoloski muzej (Archaeological Museum)
Bozidara Petranovica b.b.
57000 Zadar
☎ 058/23–950, 25–340
Open: in season from 8am–12noon and from 6–8pm, on Sunday from 8am–12noon, closed on Monday.

Stalna izlozba crkvene umetnosti (Museum of Church Art)
Stomorica b.b.
57000 Zadar
☎ 057/23–404, 23–977
Open: from 9am–12noon and from 4–6pm, closed on Monday.

Riznica-Pinakoteka Sv. Frane (Monastery of St Franciscus) (St Francis)
Trg Franje i Lucijana Vranskog 1
57000 Zadar
☎ 057/25–525
Open: every day from 9am-noon and from 5–7pm.

Travelling to Yugoslavia

By Air
See page 198.
JAT (Yugoslav Airlines) (see Useful Addresses) links up Belgrade, Ljubljana, Zagreb and other international airports in Yugoslavia with the most important cities in Europe, North America, N. Africa, Australia and the Near East, including (in Britain) Birmingham, Glasgow, London and Manchester; in the USA Cleveland, Detroit, and New York and in Canada: Montreal and Toronto.

JAT has representatives in all major towns in Yugoslavia and over forty representatives abroad. Besides JAT a large number of foreign airline companies carries out regular flights to Yugoslavia, including BA and Pan Am.

There are other airline companies in Yugoslavia — Inex Adria Aviopromet and Aviogenex and Air Yugoslavia. They mainly carry out charter flights. A number of airline companies from Britain also organise special charter flights to Yugoslavia.

By Boat
See page 198.
The Jadrolinija (Yugoslav Sea Traffic Company) (see Useful Addresses) operates along the Adriatic coast and links the main tourist centres of Rijeka, Zadar, Split, Dubrovnik and others as well as the tourist resorts and numerous islands.Ferry boats linking the Yugoslav Adriatic coast with Italian and Greek ports operate on the following lines:
Ancona — Zadar (Jadrolinija)
Bari—Bar—Bari (Prekoceanska plovidba company from Bar)
Ancona—Split—Stari Grad—Vela Luka (Jadrolinija)
Igoumenitza—Corfu—Bar—Dubrovnik (Jadrolinija)
Rijeka—Rab—Zadar—Split—Hvar—Korcula—Dubrovnik—Bar—Corfu—Igoumenitza (Jadrolinija)
Pula—Mali Losinj—Zadar (Marina of the Losinjska plovidba)
Venice—Dubrovnik, Venice—Split, Trieste—Zadar, Trieste—Split, Venice—Dubrovnik, Rimini—Zadar, Rimini—Split, Rimini—Dubrovnik, Ancona—Zadar, Ancona—Split, Ancona—Dubrovnik, Pescara—Split, Bari—Split, Bari—Dubrovnik (Italian ferry boats).

By Bus
See page 199.
Yugoslavia is linked with neighbouring countries by both regular and seasonal bus routes. Direct bus services link Yugoslavia with almost all neighbouring countries (Italy, Austria, the Federal German Republic, Switzerland, Hungary, Rumania, Bulgaria, France, Turkey).

By Rail
See page 199. The following trains travel on international lines:
Simplon Express: (London)—Paris—Milan—Belgrade
Venice Express: Venice—Belgrade—(Sofia—Istanbul)—Athens
Acropolis: Munich—Ljubljana—Belgrade—Kosovo Polje—Skopje—Athens

Tauern Express:
(London)—Ostend—Aachen—
Cologne—Munich—Zagreb—
Knin—Split
Yugoslavia Express:
Frankfurt—Munich—Ljubljana—
Zagreb—Belgrade
Hellas Express: Dortmund—
Munich—Belgrade—
Skopje—Athens; in winter also
Dortmund—Istanbul
Istanbul Express: Munich—
Belgrade—Sofia—Istanbul in
summer
Mostar—Dalmacija Express:
Stuttgart—Munich—
Zagreb—Sarajevo—Kardeljevo
and Zagreb—Knin—Split
Balkan Express: Vienna—
Maribor—Zagreb—Belgrade
Ljubljana Express: Vienna—
Maribor—Ljubljana—Rijeka
Slavija: Vienna—Maribor—
Zagreb—Belgrade
Fast train: Hamburg—Linz—
Graz—Maribor—Zagreb (Belgrade)
Polonia Express:
(Berlin—Prague)—Warsaw—
Budapest—Subotica—Belgrade—
Sofia
Pushkin: Moscow—(Budapest)—
Belgrade
Meridian: (Malmö—Berlin—
Prague—Budapest—Belgrade
Maestral: Budapest—Zagreb—
(Split), in summer
Fast train: (Turin—Venice—
Ljubljana—Zagreb
Fast train: (Rome—Venice)—
Trieste—Ljubljana
Fast train: Zürich—Ljubljana—
Zagreb—Belgrade
Fast train: Bucharest—
Timisoara—Vrsac—Belgrade.

During the summer season the
following trains also run:

Adriatica: Bratislava—
Budapest—Zagreb—Rijeka
Fast train: Munich—Rijeka (once
a week)
Jadran: Vienna—Rijeka (once a
week)
Biokovo: Vienna—Split (once a
week)

During the summer season car-
ferry trains also run:
Hamburg—Ljubljana—Koper
Düsseldorf—Ljubljana
s'Hertogenbosch—Ljubljana
Schaerbeeck (Brussels)—Ljubljana

During the season and when there
is heavy winter traffic special trains
are introduced in accordance with
requirements on certain international and domestic lines.

There are sleeping cars,
couchettes, dining and buffet cars
on international and domestic
trains linking many of Yugoslavia's
tourist centres and large towns with
major European cities.

Passenger cars can be transported by train in Yugoslavia, on a
considerable number of routes. For
detailed information contact major
railway stations or travel agencies.

All the Adriatic coast is not fully
covered by the railway network but
many towns have rail connections
with the interior (Pula, Koper,
Rijeka, Zadar, Sibenik, Split,
Kardeljevo, Bar)

Discounts
Children under the age of 4 years
who do not require a special seat

are transported free and children under 12 who require a seat travel at a discount of 50 per cent. Groups of ten or more adults travel at a discount of 25 per cent and groups of ten or more students or young people travel at a 30 per cent discount. For the hire of a special train a minimum of 300 people is required and they would travel at a discount of 30 per cent. Special rebates — INTER RAIL JUNIOR, RAIL EUROPE SENIOR and FAMILY TRAVEL are valid on international railway lines in Yugoslavia. Railway documents for Yugoslav railways are obtainable at travel agencies and stations in all major cities of Europe.

Travelling Within Yugoslavia

By Bus

Bus services within Yugoslavia are extremely well developed and all tourist resorts can be reached by a regular and frequent service. Tourist centres and towns inland are linked by express buses and during summer there are many extra services.

Motoring in Yugoslavia

See also page 201.

Accidents and Repair

There are authorised service stations in Yugoslavia for most makes of cars, but as a rule, they are to be found only in larger towns and tourist resorts. Nevertheless, motorists are advised to carry the normal essential spare parts.

The Automobile Association has an organised service for assistance and information on the roads and in towns. This service has a large number of specialised vehicles for repairing and towing motorcars. Vehicles and mechanics are stationed at over 170 bases. In case of breakdown, a specialised vehicle can be called by telephone or with the assistance of a police patrol or a passing motorist. The assistance-information bases are open from 8am to 8pm.

The introduction of a single number, **987**, for the assistance-and-information service is being introduced and the Automobile Association bases may be contacted at this number in the following towns: Backa Topola, Banja Luka, Bar, Beograd, Bihac, Bijelo Polje, Bitola, Bor Brcko, Budva, Buje, Celje, Cetinje, Crikvenica, Cacak, Cakovec, Daruvar, Delnice, Doboj, Dubrovnik, Dakovica, Durdevac, Gevgelija, Gornji Milanovac, Gospic, Ivangrad, Jastrebarsko, Kardeljevo, Karlovac, Kavadarci, Kicevo, Knin, Koper, Kotor, Kragujevac, Kraljevo, Kranj, Krapina, Krusevac, Kumanovo, Kutina, Leskovac, Ljubljana, Makarska, Maribor, Mostar, Niksic, Nis, Nova Gorica, Novi Sad, Novska, Ohrid, Osijek, Otocac, Otocec ob Krki, Pancevo, Pazin, Pirot, Pljevlja, Porec, Postojna, Pozarevac, Prijepolje, Prilep, Pristina, Prizren, Prokuplje, Pula, Rijeka, Sarajevo, Senj, Sisak, Skopje, Slavonska Pozega, Slavonski Brod, Smederevo, Sombor, Split, Sremska Mitrovica, Strumica, Subotica, Svetozarevo, Sabac, Sibenik, Titograd, Titova Mitrovica, Titovo Uzice,

Travnik, Trebinje, Tuzla, Ulcinj, Valjevo, Varazdin, Vinkovci, Virovitica, Vukovar, Zadar, Zagreb, Zajecar, Zenica, Zrenjanin, Zvornik, Zupanja, etc.

The other bases of the service still have individual numbers.

Private garages and commercial organisations also offer repair and towing services. It is advisable to get an estimate before leaving a car for repairs.

If a spare part is unavailable, an urgent order can be made through the Automobile Association (if motorists are members of foreign motoring or touring clubs).

LEGAL ASSISTANCE. Members of foreign motoring and touring clubs may get legal advice from lawyers who are associated with the Automobile Association and who are available in all the larger towns. (A list of these lawyers may be obtained from the motoring association).

LETTERS OF CREDIT. Members of foreign motoring or touring clubs who are in possession of an ETI (Entraide touring internationale) and AAI (Assistance automobile internationale) assistance booklets may use letters of credit to pay for car repairs and other services listed in the assistance booklet.

Frontier Crossings

Yugoslavia may be entered by car through the following frontier crossing points:

FROM ITALY: San Bartolomeo – Lazaret, Albaro Vescova – Skofije, Pese-Kozina, Lipizza – Lipica, Fernetti – Fernetici (Sezana), Gorizia – Nova Gorica, St Andrea – Vrtojba, Stupizza – Robic, Uccea – Uceja, Passo del Predil – Predel, Fusine Laghi – Ratece;

FROM AUSTRIA: Wurzenpass (Villach) – Korensko Sedio, Loibl-tunnel – Ljubelj, Seebergsattel – Jezersko, Grablach – Holmec, Rabenstein – Vic, Eibiswald – Radlje ob Dravi, Langegg – Jurij, Spielfeld – Sentilj, Müreck – Trate, Sicheldorf – Gederovci, Radkersburg – Gornja Radgona, Bonisdorf – Kuzma;

FROM HUNGARY: Bajánsenye – Hodos, Redics – Dolga Vas, Letenye – Gorican, Berzence – Gola, Barcs – Terezino Polje, Drávaszabolcs – Donji Miholjac, Udvar – Knezevo, Hercegszanto – Backi Breg (Bezdan), Tompa – Kelebija, Röszke – Horgos;

FROM RUMANIA: Jimbolia – Srpska Crnja, Stamora Moravita – Vatin, Naidas – Kaluderovo (Bela Crkva), Portile de Fier (Turnu Severin) – Derdap (Kladovo);

FROM BULGARIA: Kalotina – Gradina (Dimitrovgrad), Kjustendil – Deve Bair (Kriva Palanka);

FROM GREECE: Doirani – Stari Dojran, Evzoni – Bogorodica (Gevgelija), Nikki – Medzitlija;

FROM ALBANIA: Podgradec – Cafa San (Struga), Kukës – Vrbnica, Han i Hotit – Bozaj.

Motor Fuel Coupons

Motoring tourists with foreign licence plates may purchase fuel with special tourist coupons issued by Auto-moto Federation of Yugoslavia (AMSJ). These coupons can only be purchased abroad or at Yugoslav frontier points entitle holders to 5 per cent more fuel at all filling stations in Yugoslavia than the value indicated on the coupon. For further information, contact the Yugoslav National Tourist Board office.

Three grades of motor fuel are available: Premium 86 octane, Superior 98 octane and leadfree 95 octane.

Rules and Regulations
In addition to the rules and regulations outlined on page 206ff drivers must observe the following:
1. The permissible level of alcohol in blood is 0.5⁰/₀₀.
2. Drivers of heavy vehicles are forbidden to drive the vehicle for longer than 8 hours in the course of 24 hours, or cover over 500 km in the course of 24 hours.

Accommodation

Camping
See page 210. A list of camping sites is available from the Yugoslav National Tourist Board.

Hotels, Pensions and Tourist Villages
See page 209.
Hotels are classified into several categories: L (de luxe), A,B,C and D and pensions into 1st, 2nd, 3rd class. Establishments which are not of the set standard are classed as inns. For stays of more than 3 days, hotels and pensions have fixed prices which include accommodation, 3 meals a day. A list of hotels is available from the Yugoslav National Tourist office.

Motels
Over 150 motels have been built in

recent years along main roads and at the approaches to towns. Here motorists can obtain fuel, spares and repairs.

Visitors Tax
Tourists are charged this tax regardless of the kind of accommodation they use, including camping sites. Hotels and tourist offices collect the tax which averages from 12 to 60 (1986) dinars depending on local regulations and depending on the season.

Winter Holidays
The Adriatic coast has a mild climate and is very pleasant for a holiday during the winter. At many well known resorts there are air-conditioned indoor pools, thermal baths and health institutions. At Portoroz, Porec, Rovinj, Pula, Opatija, Crikvenica, Krk, Rab, Mali Losinj, Zadar, Sibenik, Primosten, Trogir, Split, Hvar, Korcula, Makarska, Dubrovnik, Cavtat, Hercegnovi and Budva comfortable hotels are open throughout the winter months and prices are exceptionally low.

Youth and Student Accommodation
There is a special organisation which deals with holidays and travel for young people and students in Yugoslavia. Karavan-Naromtravel (The organisation for international and domestic youth travel) (see Useful Addresses), 11000 Belgrade, has its own international youth centres in Dubrovnik, Rovinj, Becici (near Budva) and Kopaonik with suitable accommodation and entertainments for young people. During the summer

Naromtravel organises charter flights from Yugoslavia to various towns in Europe as well as package holidays. Naromtravel also specialises in the organisation of study and tourist trips throughout Yugoslavia, special interest programmes, accommodation, winter holidays, etc. Karavan Naromtravel is a member of ISTC, FIYTO, SATA, BITEJ and is authorised to issue ISIC, YIEE and IUS cards.

To book, apply direct to Karavan-Naromtravel at the above address or to tour operators or travel agencies who include these trips in the programme.

Accommodation for young people is also available in the organisation of the Yugoslav Youth School Organisation (Ferijaini Savez) which has a large number of hotels. There are students' hotels in the large towns and some schools are also used during the summer.

Tips for Travellers

Currency
See page 205. Foreign currency may be exchanged for dinars or dinar cheques. *Dinar cheques* offer some advantages: only unused dinar cheques can be reconverted into foreign currency and these cheques entitle the holder to a discount of 5–10 per cent when paying for services in many big hotels and restaurants wherever there is a sign to this effect.

Customs Regulations
See also page 205. In addition to the limitations outlined in *Advice to Tourists*, the following should also be observed:

1. Those in possession of radio equipment, weapons and ammunition are obliged to report this to the Yugoslav frontier authorities at the point of entry. Those in possession of a radio must acquire a utilisation permit in advance (apply to consulars).

2. It is necessary for a dog or cat to have a veterinary certificate to prove that it has been vaccinated against rabies and that not less than 15 days or more than 6 months have elapsed since the day of vaccination.

Medical Care
See also page 206. While staying in Yugoslavia, foreigners are entitled to medical care and may use medical services of any hospital. British citizens are entitled to free medical care when needed (against payment of a minimal fee). American and Canadian citizens are advised to take out short-term medical cover.

National Holidays
1, 2 January; 1, 2 May; 4 July; 29, 30 November in all Yugoslavia. In Serbia, 7 July; in Montenegro 13 July; Slovenia 27 April, 22 July, 1 November; Croatia 27 July; Bosnia and Hercegovina 27 July, 25 November; Macedonia 2 August, 11 October.

Passports/Visas
See page 207. Foreigners of countries with which Yugoslavia has diplomatic or consular relations coming to Yugoslavia as tourists

may spend 30 days in Yugoslavia with a *Tourist Pass* issued on the basis of a valid passport or or identity card at all frontier crossings open for international traffic. A *Tourist Pass* cannot be extended. Tourists who are holders of a valid passport using a *Tourist Pass* for their stay in Yugoslavia may extend their stay by applying for a visa at the local internal affairs authorities. The fee for the *Tourist Pass* is nominal.

Radio

Radio Yugoslavia broadcasts daily programmes for foreign tourists in ten languages.

Programmes in English are broadcast at 3.30pm, 6.30pm, 8.00pm and 10.15pm GMT. The wavelengths are 19.46, 19.69, 25.56, 31.19, 41.44, 49.18m.

Souvenirs

Yugoslavia has a long tradition of handicrafts: In all the large towns there are 'Narodna radinost' (Folk Crafts) shops selling handmade embroidery, fine lace, leather articles, filigree jewellery, carpets, ceramics, national costumes etc.

Tourist Information Offices in Yugoslavia

Regional and Main Offices

Bosnia–Hercogovina
Turisticki savez Bosne i Hercegovine
Titova 80
Sarajevo

Central Tourist Office
Turisticki savez Jugoslavije
Mose Pijade 18/IV
Beograd

Croatia
Turisticki savez Hrvatske
Amruseva 8
Zagreb

Dubrovnik
Turisticki informativni centar
P. Milicevica 1

Macedonia
Turisticki savez makedonije
Marsala Tita 99
Skopje

Montenegro
Turisticki savez Crne Gore
Bulevar Lenjina 2
Titograd

Rijeka
Turisticki informativni biro
Trg Republike 9
Rijeka 51000
☎ 33–909

Serbia
Turisticki savez Srjbije
Dobrinjska 11
Beograd

Slovenia
Turisticki savez Stovenije
Miklosiceva Cesta 38/V1
Ljubljana

Split
Turisticki biro Split
Titova Obala 12
☎ 42–142

Other Tourist Information Centres

Beograd
The subway at Terazije street, next to the Albania Building
11000 Belgrade
☎ 635–343/635–622

Dubrovnik
Placa 1
50000 Dubrovnik
☎ 263–54/263–55

Pula
Trg bratstva i jedinstra 4
52000 Pula
☎ 34–355

Sarajevo
JNA 50
71000 Sarajevo
☎ 25–151

Titograd
ul. Slobode 43
81000 Titograd
☎ 52–968

Useful Addresses

Accommodation

(Organisation for international and domestic youth travel)
Knez Mihailova 50
11000 Beograd
☎ 011/187822

Advice and Information

British Embassy
General Zdanova 46
Beograd
☎ 645–055

British Consulate General
Ilica 12
Zagreb
☎ 424–888

British Consulate
Titova Obala
Split
☎ 41–464

Canadian Embassy
Kneza Milosa 75
Beograd
☎ 644–666

Consulate General of the SFR of Yugoslavia
17th Floor
767 Third Avenue
New York
NY 10017
☎ (212) 838–2300

Consulate General of the SFR of Yugoslavia
Suite 1600
307 North Michigan Avenue
60601 Illinois
☎ 332–0169/ 332–0170

Consulate General of the SFR of Yugoslavia
Suite 1605
625 Stanwix Street
Pittsburgh
Pennsylvania 15222
☎ 471–6191

Consulate General of the SFR of Yugoslavia
Suite 406
1375 Sutter Street
San Francisco
California 94709
☎ 776–4941/2/3

Consulate of the SFR of
Yugoslavia
Suite 4R
Park Centre 1700 E
13th Street
Cleveland
Ohio 44114
☎ 621–2094/612–2093

Consulate General of the SFR of
Yugoslavia
377 Spadine Road
Toronto
Ontario
M5P 2V7
☎ 481–7279

Economic Chamber of Yugoslavia
Knez Mihailova
11000 Belgrade

Embassy of the SFR of Yugoslavia
Consular Section
5–7 Lexham Gardens
London W8 5JU
☎ (01) 370–6105/9

US Consulate General
Bracé Kavurica 2
Zagreb
☎ 444–800

US Embassy
Kneza Milosa 50
Beograd
☎ 645–655

Yugoslav National Tourist Office
143 Regent Street
London W1
☎ (01) 439–0399/734–5243

Yugoslav National Tourist Office
Suite 210, Rockefeller Center,
630 Fifth Avenue
New York
NY 10020
☎ (212) 757–2801

Motoring Organisations

AMSJ
(Auto-moto savez Jugoslavije)
Ruzveltova 18
11000 Beograd
☎ 401–699

Auto-moto savez Bosne i
Hercegovine
Borise Kovacevica 18
71000 Sarajevo
☎ 24–292

Auto-moto savez Hrvatske
Draskoviceva 25
41000 Zagreb
☎ 415–023

Auto-moto savez Crne Gore
Novaka Miloseva 12/11
81000 Titograd
☎ 44–467

Auto-moto
Slovenije
Titova Cesta 138
61000 Ljubljana
☎ 342–661

Auto-moto savez Makedonije
Ivo Ribar Lola 51
91000 Skopje
☎ 226–825

Auto-moto savez Srbije
Ivana Milutinovica 58
11000 Beograd
☎ 4443–905

Auto-Moto savez Kosova
Magistralni put 1
38000 Pristina
☎ 43–555

Sport and Leisure

(Diving and Snorkelling)
Savez za sportski ribolov na moru i
podvone aktivnosti SFRJ
Matije Gupca 2
Rijeka

(Yugoslav Hunting Association)
Savez lovackih organizacija
Jugoslavije
Alekse Nenadovica 23
Beograd

Travel

JAT (Yugoslav Airlines)
Bircarvinova 1
Beograd
☎ 642–453/643–384 (international
flights)
☎ 131–392/332–179 (domestic
flights)

Jadrolinija
(Yugoslav Sea Traffic Company)
Obala jugoslovenske mornarice 16
Rijeka
☎ 051/24–051

Telephones

Dialling Codes
To the UK from Yugoslavia **99 44**
+ area code

To US and Canada from Yugoslavia **99 1** + area code
To Yugoslavia from the US and
Canada **011 38** + area code
To Yugoslavia from the UK **010
38** + area code

Area Codes
Belgrade (Beograd) **11**
Dubrovnik **50**
Rijeka **51**
Sarajevo **71**
Split **58**
Titograd **81**
Zadar **57**
Zagreb **41**

How to Use Pay Phones
Use the silver 2, 5 or 10 dinar
coins.
Pick up the receiver.
Deposit coins, wait for dial tone.
Dial number.
There are reduced rates for long-
distance and international calls on
Sundays.

Useful Numbers
Police (emergency) **92** or **94**
AMSJ (Yugoslav Motoring
Organisation) **987**
Emergency medical aid **94**
Fire brigade **92** or **93**
Local information **981**
Local directory assistance **988**
Long distance and international
operator **981**

INDEX

Index to Places

Index to Subjects